AN ORGANIC HANDB

Controlling
WEEDS
without using chemicals

JO READMAN

the organic
organisation

HDRA/Search Press

Published in Great Britain 2000

Search Press Ltd
Wellwood, North Farm Road,
Tunbridge Wells, Kent TN2 3DR

in association with

HDRA
Ryton Organic Gardens
Coventry CV8 3LG

Originally published as *Weeds: how to control them and love them* in 1991

Illustrations by Polly Pinder
Photographs by Charlotte de la Bedoyère

The publishers would like to thank: Pat Donovan of The Sussex Botanical Recording Society for her assistance in the identification of the weeds and for the photograph of coltsfoot on page 25; John Fisher for the photograph of corn spurrey on page 35; Arthur Hoare for the photograph of shepherd's needle on page 33; Jo Readman for the photographs of enchanter's nightshade on page 13, horsetail on page 15, lesser celandine on page 21, comfrey on page 23 and wild pansy on page 37.

ISBN 0 85532 934 3

Conversion Chart

From centimetres to inches		*From grammes to ounces*	
1 cm	= ½ in	7 g =	¼ oz
2.5 cm	= 1 in	14 g =	½ oz
5 cm	= 2 in	28 g =	1 oz
10 cm	= 4 in	110 g =	4 oz
50 cm	= 20 in	450 g =	16 oz (1 lb)
100 cm (1 m)	= 40 in	*From litres to pints*	
1 sq m	= 1.2 sq yds	1 l = 1.75 pt	

Exact conversions from imperial to metric measures are not possible, so the metric measures have been rounded up.

Printed in Spain by Elkar S. Coop, 48180 Loiu (Bizkaia)

Introduction

A weed is most commonly described as a plant in the wrong place. This could include rogue potatoes that spring up in the wrong parts of the garden, strawberry runners that creep amongst your vegetables and even vegetables that have found their way, uninvited, into the flower-beds. But, when we refer to weeds, we really think of plants like couch, chickweed, knotweed, and the dreaded dandelion.

So what makes these plants weeds? Firstly, they compete with your vegetables, flowers and lawns for light, water and food. They may also contain poisons and harbour pests and diseases. The main problem, however, is their tenacity. They are determined to stay, or return at the first opportunity. They take full advantage of your activities in the garden, quickly spreading over bare ground when you cultivate the soil.

In nature, these 'weeds' are highly successful wild plants, adapted to rapidly colonise bare ground or land that is constantly being disturbed. They are 'programmed' for survival. Some weeds can regenerate themselves from tiny pieces of root or stem. Others can produce thousands of seeds which germinate, grow, and set seed again in a few weeks.

Weeds also have many beneficial properties. Some improve the soil, some attract wildlife and predators, some can be eaten and many were used in the past for their herbal properties. Also, it is often forgotten that many of them are beautiful wild flowers in their own right. So, before you pull out the next weed, think again.

The first section of this book describes and illustrates many of the common and some of the not so common garden weeds, and looks at their properties and the way that they grow. In certain situations you have to remove weeds, so the second half of the book concentrates on how you can control weeds organically in all parts of the garden.

The ecology of weeds

If you can get to understand your weeds and how they work, then you may come to tolerate some. This understanding will also help you to control weeds effectively and organically. Weeds are successful because:
● They can spread rapidly, by seed and/or vegetatively.
● They are aggressive, fast growing and real survivors.
● They are variable and can adapt rapidly to hostile conditions.
● They grow where they will find nourishment and where their living conditions are fulfilled.
● They live in communities and not as a monoculture.
● They are, in general, more resistant to disease than crops.

Life cycles

Weeds are either annual, ephemeral, biennial or perennial.

Annuals develop from seeds which grow, flower, set seed and die in a year. See life cycle on page 6.

Ephemerals can complete several life cycles in a year. See life cycle on page 6.

Biennials complete their life cycle in two years. See life cycle on page 7.

Perennials are plants which persist for more than a year and often for many years. See life cycle on page 7.

Seeds

Many weeds, particularly annuals and ephemerals, reproduce and spread by seed. This means that they can survive changing conditions:
● Seeds ensure that the plant survives dry or cold periods.

● They can sometimes travel great distances to a more suitable site.
● Offspring may be able to live in an area that the parents could not tolerate, as they are genetically different.
● Seeds can provide a fresh start if the parent has fallen foul to a disease.

Pollination

Many weeds, such as dandelion, are 'apomictic' and can produce seed without fertilisation. Others, such as shepherd's purse, are self-fertilising. In these cases it only takes one to tango, and the plant can reproduce even when isolated.

Strength in numbers

A patch of ground as small as 30 sq cm can contain up to 5,000 seeds. Many weeds produce vast quantities of seeds.

Plant	Type	Seeds per plant
Greater plantain	Perennial	14,000
Field bindweed	Perennial	600
Sowthistle	Annual	21,000 to 25,000
Fat hen	Annual	70,000
Groundsel	Ephemeral	1,000
Chickweed	Ephemeral	2,500

Ephemerals produce less seed than annuals but have just as many offspring. Chickweed has a life cycle of only seven weeks and can produce up to 15,000 million plants a year.

Getting about

Weed seeds have evolved some fantastic ways of getting about. The opportunists take advantage of wind, water, fur, feathers, ants, bird droppings, shoes and just about anything else that you may care to mention.
● *Wind* Weeds such as dandelions and groundsel have well-engineered parachutes to give them lift. Willowherbs have hairs to catch the wind, while the tree weeds sycamore and ash have winged seeds, the 'helicopters' that many of us played with as children. Minute seeds, like those produced

Dandelion

by pearlwort, are easily spread by wind. Using these methods, sycamores have travelled up to 4 km, coltsfoot 14 km and ragwort over 100 km.

● *Inside animals* Many weed seeds can survive passing through an animal's gut, e.g. charlock, redshank, fat hen, blackberry, and may even germinate more readily when they emerge from the other end. . .keep composting that manure!

● *Outside animals* Some weed seeds, e.g. cleavers, burdock, enchanter's nightshade, come equipped with hooks or spurs to grab onto and hitch a ride from passers-by. The seeds of shepherd's purse are covered in mucilage and stick easily to birds' feet and others in wet conditions. Many seeds have oil bodies, 'elaisomes', attached to them, e.g. speedwell, spurge, annual mercury. These are sought out by ants and dragged some distance before the oil comes off.

● *Missiles* Seeds that are shot out when ripe,

e.g. oxalis, hairy bittercress, violet, ground elder, balsam, may not get very far but they do not have to rely on wind or animals. You may unwittingly give them a hand. Many a time ardent weeders spread hairy bittercress seeds when attempting to pull out its parents.

Himalayan balsam

● *Water* Any seed that can float can spread by water. The prize must, however, go to ivy-leaved toadflax. This weed grows in walls and pokes its flowers out to the sun. When the seeds are ripe, the mature head turns to the wall and releases its seeds during rain, thus ensuring that it gets a good, moist seedbed in the cracks.

Ivy-leaved toadflax

Life cycle of an annual plant

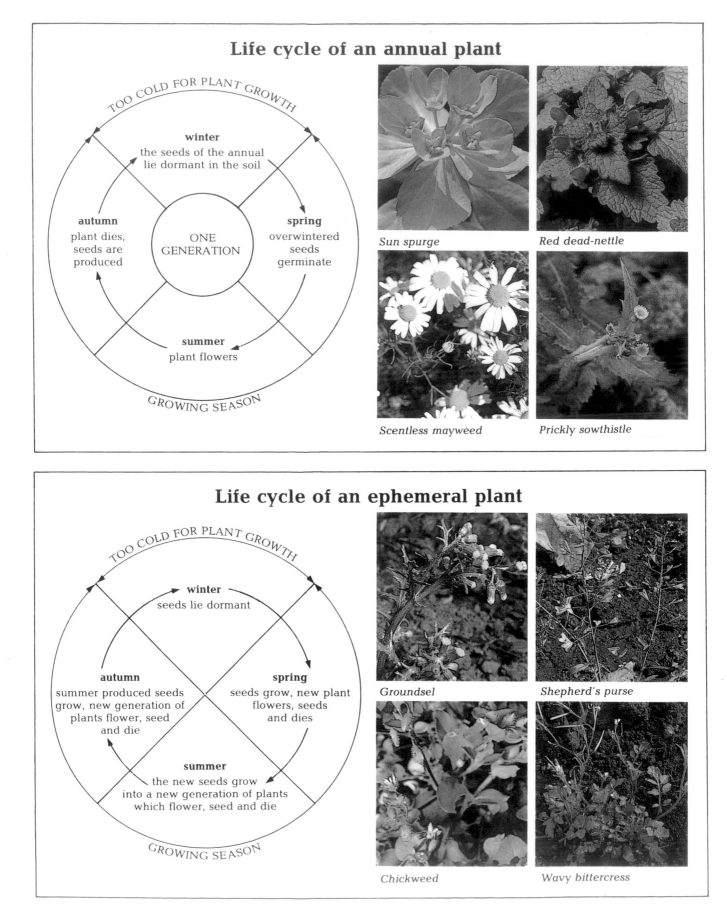

TOO COLD FOR PLANT GROWTH

winter
the seeds of the annual lie dormant in the soil

autumn
plant dies, seeds are produced

ONE GENERATION

spring
overwintered seeds germinate

summer
plant flowers

GROWING SEASON

Sun spurge

Red dead-nettle

Scentless mayweed

Prickly sowthistle

Life cycle of an ephemeral plant

TOO COLD FOR PLANT GROWTH

winter
seeds lie dormant

autumn
summer produced seeds grow, new generation of plants flower, seed and die

spring
seeds grow, new plant flowers, seeds and dies

summer
the new seeds grow into a new generation of plants which flower, seed and die

GROWING SEASON

Groundsel

Shepherd's purse

Chickweed

Wavy bittercress

Life cycle of a biennial plant

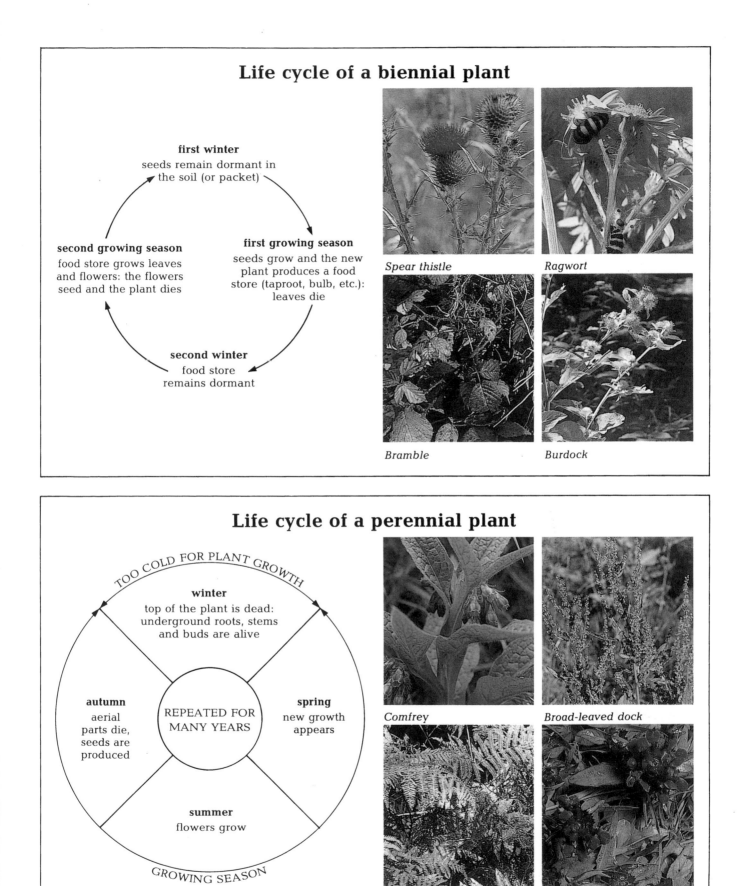

first winter
seeds remain dormant in the soil (or packet)

first growing season
seeds grow and the new plant produces a food store (taproot, bulb, etc.): leaves die

second winter
food store remains dormant

second growing season
food store grows leaves and flowers: the flowers seed and the plant dies

Spear thistle

Ragwort

Bramble

Burdock

Life cycle of a perennial plant

TOO COLD FOR PLANT GROWTH

winter
top of the plant is dead: underground roots, stems and buds are alive

spring
new growth appears

REPEATED FOR MANY YEARS

autumn
aerial parts die, seeds are produced

summer
flowers grow

GROWING SEASON

Comfrey

Broad-leaved dock

Bracken

Self-heal

Lying in wait

Not all seeds germinate immediately and there is always a big reserve of dormant seeds in the soil: the 'seed bank'. Knotgrass can stay dormant for up to sixty years and poppies for over one hundred. Some go dormant if it is too hot, e.g. chickweed, or if they are too deep. Others contain chemicals which need to be washed out, or have a tough seed coat that needs time to soften and absorb water. Many weed seeds need light to germinate and spring into life when they are brought to the surface. They can even detect different wavelengths of light and will not germinate in the light that filters through overshadowing vegetation. Some weeds can germinate at any time of year, e.g. annual meadow-grass, some germinate in the autumn and overwinter as rosettes, e.g. shepherd's purse, while others wait until spring, e.g. fool's parsley. Some weed seeds can even plant themselves; wild oats, when moistened promptly, up-end and drill themselves into the ground!

Seeds

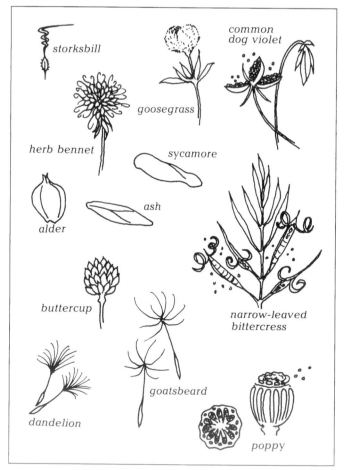

storksbill

common dog violet

goosegrass

herb bennet

sycamore

alder

ash

buttercup

narrow-leaved bittercress

goatsbeard

dandelion

poppy

Vegetative spread

Although many perennials produce seeds, their main way of spreading is usually vegetatively. Reproducing by seed ensures survival for the future when conditions may change, but vegetative reproduction ensures survival in the present. As the plant spreads it can still obtain food from its well-established parent. It is still attached to the apron strings. Weeds spread vegetatively using: creeping stems above the ground – stolons and runners; creeping stems below the ground – rhizomes; creeping horizontal roots.

Stolon

This is a long branch that bends towards the ground. Blackberry stolons root as their stems bend earthwards, even before they touch the ground. It is a very effective and rapid way of spreading. In New Zealand they say that there are two blackberry plants; one on the North Island and one on the South Island!

Rhizomes

These underground stems are produced by many weeds and are something that are all too familiar. Plants producing rhizomes include couch, nettle, ground elder, coltsfoot, hedge bindweed, horsetail and Japanese knotweed. They usually grow close to the surface and have dormant buds along their length. If the growing point at the end is snapped off, then the dormant buds leap into life and send up new shoots.

Roots

Plants like creeping thistle (see illustration on page 13) and perennial sowthistle produce horizontal roots which act in the same way as rhizomes. These roots can produce new buds at any position along their length and send up new plants (see illustration of dandelion taproot on page 10). Field bindweed (*Convulvulus*) can spread 25 sq m a season, its roots growing unseen below the surface.

Couch rhizome

Couch

Runner

This is a creeping stem that comes from a bud and runs along the ground. Plantlets are found at each node and quickly send down roots to get established. Using this method, creeping buttercup can spread 3 sq m a season and cinquefoil 10 sq m! Cinquefoil can produce up to 15 runners per plant and each one can have up to 20 plantlets on it. On top of that, the plant also produces flowers and seeds in sunny conditions. Some annuals, e.g. chickweed, knotgrass, common field speed-well, are also prostrate creepers and produce flowers along their length, seeding as they go.

Creeping buttercup runner

Blackberry stolon

9

Regeneration

Most perennial weeds are determined to stay and can regenerate themselves from small pieces of root or rhizome. In these cases, digging a plot of land can fragment the stems and roots and lead to a whole new population of weeds. Even some annuals, such as knotgrass, can regenerate themselves if cut back.

Taproots

Plants with taproots, such as dock and dandelion, have no natural vegetative spread but rapidly regenerate themselves when cut up. In addition, both these weeds produce vast quantities of seed which help them to spread. Taproots have an added advantage. They can help the plant survive unfavourable conditions as they contain food reserves and can tap the soil at great depths.

Dandelion rosette

Yet more survival tactics

Many weeds can survive adverse weather conditions, being trampled on, attempts to eat them, and can even change shape to fit in with their surroundings.

Many annual weed seeds are very hardy. Groundsel and chickweed seeds can survive prolonged periods at −9°C without a shiver. Speedwell and dead-nettle keep growing throughout the winter and even flower when it is mild. The deep rooters, such as dock and dandelion, can tolerate drought and still look happy and green when the grass begins to look crispy and vegetables droop. Weeds like plantain, dandelion and daisy positively thrive from being walked on. These plants damage lawns and have a growing point below the reach of the mower blades which keeps them out of harm's way. They all produce rosettes of leaves that sit close to the surface and smother out the grass beneath them. If you do not mow the lawn, then the plantains and dandelions take on another form and rapidly grow up towards the sky to reach the light. Other weeds use whatever they can to do the same. Cleavers and bindweeds scramble upwards in the race to get to the best position. As well as being aggressive, many species defend themselves rigorously with prickles, stings and spines. Hemlock, ragwort, henbane and deadly nightshade are amongst the poisonous ones. Even clover has a sting in its tail. It contains two chemicals which, when mixed, form a deadly cocktail: cyanide!

Dandelion taproot

Know your weeds

Now take a look at some of the weeds that you find in your garden. Despite their tenacity they are not all bad! The height of each of the weeds listed here is described using the terms tall (over 60 cm), medium (30 to 60 cm), short (10 to 30 cm) and low (0 to 10 cm). However, these should be used as a general guide only, as factors such as weather conditions, soil and light will all affect a plant's growth.

Perennials
This section includes biennials and perennials

Achillea millefolium
Yarrow

A common lawn weed in the daisy family. Feathery leaves, with white or pinkish flowers in flat umbel-like clusters from June to November. Reproduces by seed, and roots at the nodes of creeping flat stems, spreading 7 to 20 cm a year. Said to be used by Achilles to cure wounds caused by iron. Old wound herb used to treat injured soldiers. Compost activator. Once used as a cleansing agent in beer. Contains an alkaloid thought to taint butter if consumed in large quantities by cows.

Yarrow

Ground elder

Aegopodium podagraria
Ground elder
(Bishop's weed, Jack jump about, goutwort.)

A nightmare in many gardens. Umbellifer with white flowers from July to August. A vigorous weed, growing up to 1 m a year from spreading underground rhizomes. Also spread by seeds which shed in all directions when the ripe heads are touched.
Introduced from the Mediterranean during the Middle Ages and cultivated in monastery gardens as a herb to cure gout, a complaint associated with high-living bishops. Dedicated to Saint Gerard, patron saint of gout sufferers! Nice spinach-like vegetable if cooked in butter. A sedative and kidney-flushing herb.

Burdock

Arctium spp.
Burdock
Found on all soils, on waste ground and around old buildings.

Arctium lappa
Greater burdock
(Foxes cloat, love leaves, beggar's buttons.)

Large, with blunt leaves. Spread by animals, the hooked fruits easily sticking to fur and clothing. The stripped stems can be boiled and served with butter. A lotion prepared from the roots was said to cure baldness. Burdock is rich in minerals and vitamins and was used medicinally to cleanse the blood and as a diuretic. Food for painted lady butterfly larvae.

Arctium minus
Lesser burdock
Medium/tall, downy biennial with heart-shaped leaves. Egg-shaped purple flowers found from July to September.

Bellis perennis
Daisy
(Day's eye, Bessy banewood, hen and chickens, bruisewort, cat posy, sweeps.)

Weed of lawns but can spread to cultivated ground, especially if lawn mowings used as a mulch. Spoon-shaped leaves. Flower-head contains many yellow flowers surrounded by white rays, found from March to October. Shoots, in the axils of leaves, spread the rosettes which are often found on lawns. Ants can help to spread the plant's seeds too.

Makes a mild insecticide as it has an acid secretion disliked by many insects. Daisy water was used by gypsies to cure red blotches on the skin. Also, once used against varicose veins, open sores, and other aches and pains. Wine can be made from the flowers which open during the day and close at night.

Daisy

Calystegia sepium
Hedge bindweed
(Bearbine, ropewind, woodbine, hedge lily, old man's nightcap.)

Smothers plants as it climbs over them. Climbing plant with heart-shaped leaves and large white flowers found from June to September.

Spreads by its deep roots which can grow a whole new plant when broken off. Often found in damp soils, in hedges and on shrubs. Has poisonous sap. (See *Convulvulus arvensis*, page 14.)

Chelidonium majus
Greater celandine
(Swallowwort, tetterwort.)

A weed of the poppy family. Native of Southern Europe and Asia and naturalised in Britain.

Hairless branched stem that gives a poisonous orange juice when snapped open. Leaves greyish and lobed. Yellow flowers, in clusters of three to eight, open from April when the swallows arrive until October when they leave.

Grown in the Middle Ages for medicinal purposes, such as removing warts and curing eye ailments and jaundice. Do not try this now as the juice has been found to contain poisonous alkaloids. The plant was once boiled in water and given to turkeys to prevent diarrhoea; charming!

Circaea lutetiana
Enchanter's nightshade

A member of the fuchsia family which is difficult to get rid of once established. Simple opposite leaves. White flowers found on a long spike which gets longer before the flowers fall.

The fruits are covered with glistening hooked bristles which stick easily to gardeners and animals, spreading them far and wide. The plant also produces fleshy underground shoots which pop up as new plants all around the parent when it dies.

Enchanter's nightshade

Creeping thistle

Cirsium arvense
Creeping thistle
(Dashel, dodger, boar thistle, cursed thistle.)

This weed creeps up behind your back if you leave even just a little plant in the garden. Stems are not spiky like the leaves. Lilac coloured flowers are found from June to September and smell lovely, attracting bees and butterflies. This thistle does not form a rosette like its relatives.

The seeds of creeping thistle are carried great distances on the wind. The plant also has a taproot of 2.5 to 3 cm which produces lateral roots, each sending up a new plant. Using this method it can spread up to 12 m a year! Even when broken the root fragments can throw up new plants.

Leaves can be used around crop plants to keep off slugs but the plant is host to the bean aphis and celery fly so it is best kept out of the garden. This thistle can tolerate up to 2% salt so the salt pot, often used to control lawn weeds, will not eradicate it.

Cirsium vulgare
Spear thistle
(Bow thistle, bur, quat vessel.)

Can be distinguished from creeping thistle because it forms a rosette and often has solitary flowers. A biennial, it spreads by seed. Some ground beetle larvae eat the seeds so they should be encouraged and not regarded as foes.

Spear thistle

Convulvulus arvensis
Field bindweed
(Hellweed, devil's guts.)

The common names of this weed certainly reflect the gardener's opinion of it as it scrambles over plants and strangles them. A creeping and climbing plant with smaller flowers than hedge bindweed. The flowers, which are white or pink and slightly perfumed, are found from June to September. They shut in the dark and when rain is forecast.

The plant creeps above and below ground with roots like a mass of white spaghetti that go down several feet. It is difficult to get rid of as each root fragment grows into a new plant. This plant indicates a deep, fertile soil and is popular with bees and the white plume moth.

Field bindweed

Dipsacus fullonum
Teasel

Leaves form a rosette and are covered in white pimples. The leaves wither before flowering in July and August. The beautiful conical spike of purple flowers is attractive to bees and goldfinches. After flowering, the stems and flower-heads remain and were once used for carding wool.

Teasel

Elymus repens
Couch
(Twitch, Scotch squelch.)

A very persistent garden weed. Forms tufts or large patches of dull green leaves. Sends up spikes of green flowers and seeds.

Couch is very aggressive and spreads rapidly with its underground rhizomes. These underground stems have hard, ivory coloured tips that can grow right through plants such as potatoes. Even very small pieces of rhizome can quickly give rise to a whole new plant.

However, the plant does have its uses. Cats and dogs often eat it when they feel ill. Extracts from the rhizomes have been used to treat rheumatism, gout, cystitis and kidney stones, and are renowned for their diuretic and blood-purifying properties. In Italy and France, roots have often been sold in markets and, just to make you feel better, here is a quote from Culpepper the herbalist: 'Although a gardener be of another opinion, yet a physician holds half an acre of them to be worth five acres of carrots twice over.' Oh well, each to his own.
(See illustration on page 9.)

14

Epilobium angustifolium
Rosebay willowherb
(Blitzweed, fireweed.)

An unusual weed in that it forms great clumps on its own, often on sites laid bare by fire or in damp gardens. Tall, with alternate willow-like leaves and bright pink flowers in a spike. Spreads by underground rhizomes and wind-dispersed seeds. One plant can produce up to 100,000 seeds which are carried on parachutes of long silky hairs.

Rosebay willowherb

Great willowherb

Epilobium hirsutum
Great willowherb
(Codlins and cream.)

Tall and hairy with purplish/pink flowers occurring in clumps near the top of the stem.

Epilobium montanum
Broad-leaved willowherb

Smaller than rosebay willowherb with creeping stems and pale pink flowers.

Equisetum spp.
Horsetail
(Cat's tail, feather, puddock pipes, jointweed, holy water sprinkle.)

A troublesome weed associated with damp gardens. A non-flowering, unbranched plant with brittle underground rhizomes.

The plant spreads using underground stems. These have black tubers which easily break off and re-establish themselves. *Equisetum* also spreads by spores which are produced on fruiting bodies in the spring. These give rise to a short-lived sexual generation and are the reason why the plant needs moist soil. These tiny moss-like plants produce sperm which need to swim to the female to bring about fertilisation. The familiar horsetail is then formed and the cycle continues.

Although horsetails are poisonous and difficult to eradicate they do have some benefits. They were once used as an antiseptic, to stop bleeding, and for nervous disorders, as well as for cleaning pans. An infusion of *Equisetum* in water has also been used as a spray against fungal diseases.

Horsetail

Filipendula ulmaria
Meadowsweet

(Bittersweet, bride-wort, courtship and matrimony, sweet hay, queen of the meadow.)

Favours damp sites. A tall, hairless plant with pinnate leaves and creamy, fragrant clusters of delicate flowers. Like willow, it contains salacin from which headache remedies were once made.

Meadowsweet

Glechoma hederacea
Ground ivy

Low, creeping, purplish plant with loose whorls of violet flowers at the base of leaves from March to June. Spreads rapidly by runners, carpeting the ground.

Ground ivy

Hedera helix
Ivy

A hardy, evergreen, woody climber, carpeting the ground or ascending by means of tiny roots. Glossy green leaves with tiny green and yellow flowers from September to November. A good example of a weed being a plant in the wrong place. Ivy can be a menace, attacking buildings when it grows vertically and smothering vegetables and flowers when it creeps horizontally.

Some cultivated varieties, such as 'Hedera helix-var. Gold heart', look beautiful in gardens, screening walls and climbing up posts, surviving well in the shade. However, they do need to be kept under control.

Ivy is poisonous to humans but is a useful nectar source for insects in the autumn and is often alive with bees and butterflies. It also provides shelter and accommodation for birds.

Ivy

Heracleum sphondylium
Hogweed

Tall, stout biennial/perennial up to 3 m. Pinnate leaves, with white umbels of flowers borne from April to November.

Once collected and fed to pigs, the young tips can be scraped, cooked and eaten like asparagus. Beware of the close relative of this plant, *Heracleum mantegazzianum*, which can grow 5 m tall and causes painful blisters on the skin when touched.

Hogweed

Hypochaeris radicata
Common cat's-ear

(Bent, gosmore, bennets.)

A common weed on lawns. Common cat's-ear is a medium perennial with rough, hairy, dandelion-like leaves. Solitary dandelion-like flowers are found from June to September, occasionally on branched stalks.

Can easily be confused with all the hawkbits and nipplewort (see pages 18, 30). The illustration is, in fact, of *Leontodon autumnalis* (autumn hawkbit) which closely resembles common cat's-ear.

Autumn hawkbit

Lamium album
White dead-nettle

(Archangels, sucky Sue, Adam and Eve – if the flowers are held upside-down, then the black and gold stamens look like two people asleep side by side.)

A common weed in most of Britain but rare in Scotland and Ireland. This nettle looks like stinging nettle but can be distinguished by its square stem and white flowers found from early spring to late autumn.

The plant spreads by rooting stolons and by seeds which are dispersed by ants. A good nectar source for bees. People also use the plant: the leaves can be eaten like spinach, or made into beer or tea as a remedy for a chill.

Linaria vulgaris
Common toadflax

Short/medium, hairless plant with thin pointed leaves and yellow snapdragon flowers from June to October. It tolerates stony ground and provides nectar for those insects with tongues long enough to reach inside the flower.

Common toadflax

Lotus corniculatus
Birdsfoot Trefoil

Prostrate perennial with 5 leaflets. The orange/yellow flowers are found from May to September in bunches at the top of the stems. This plant fixes nitrogen and, therefore, indicates low nitrogen levels in the soil.

Birdsfoot trefoil

Malva sylvestris
Common mallow
(Bread and cheese, fairy cheeses – on account of the leaves being eaten, rags and tatters, flibberty gibbet.)

A free garden flower. Leaves, which are high in vitamins A, B1, B2 and C were eaten in salads, and used as poultices for relieving toothache.

Ononis repens
Restharrow

A medium, semi-erect undershrub with trefoil leaves and hairy stem. The pink pea-like flowers are found from July to September.
The plant is found on dry, rough ground. Its name comes from the days when horses worked the land and they had to stop on rough ground to have tough roots from 'resting harrows' untangled. It is sometimes called 'cammocks' as it is thought to taint the milk if eaten by cows.

Pentaglottis sempervirens
Green alkanet

A garden escape originally from South West Portugal and Spain. A member of the borage family. A medium, hairy perennial with bright blue white-eyed flowers found from April to July.
The plant has a brittle deep root which regenerates itself if broken off. The stem, too, can send up new shoots and flowers if cut. Green alkanet is most common in the south west of Britain and near the coast.

Hawksbeard

Green alkanet

Pilosella officinarum
Mouse-ear hawkweed

A common lawn weed that is really troublesome when established. Short, creeping plant covered in fine white hairs. Dandelion-like flowers are produced from May to October. Common on light, dry soils.
It overwinters as a rosette of small hairy leaves. In spring, stolons appear from the base of the plant, each terminating in a new rosette. These form a mat on the lawn and smother out the grass. The plant also spreads to new sites by seed.
There are many, many plants in the daisy family with dandelion-like flowers, many of which are lawn weeds, and it is beyond the scope of this book to identify them all.
Species with similar habits which may also be found in the garden include:
Crepis biennis – Rough hawksbeard,
Crepis capillaris – Smooth hawksbeard,
Hieracium umbellatum – Leafy hawkweed,
Hypochaeris radicata – Common cat's-ear,
Leontodon hispidus – Rough hawkbit,
Leontodon taraxacoides – Lesser hawkbit,
Picris echioides – Bristly ox-tongue,
Picris hieracioides – Hawkweed ox-tongue.
For further details on identification it is best to consult a good flora. Good luck!

Plantago major
Greater plantain
(Englishman's footprint, waybread, snakeweed.)

A weed of lawns and paths that thrives on being battered and walked over. The leaves have ribbed veins and are found in a basal rosette. Tiny flowers are found on leafless stalks from June to October. The seeds become sticky when wet and are dispersed by sparrows. About 15,000 seeds can be produced from one plant and some of these can remain dormant for up to forty years.

Plantain can be cooked like spinach. It is also renowned as a healing plant (hence the name 'slan us' in Scotland) and the fresh juice gives relief from stings and bites.

Greater plantain

Japanese knotweed

This aggressive weed was introduced into Britain in 1825. *The Garden*, in 1879, described it as 'a plant of sterling merit, now becoming quite common. . .and is undoubtedly one of the finest herbaceous plants in cultivation'. Today it is one of the most troublesome weeds and extremely difficult to eradicate. It is now illegal in Britain to propagate or deliberately plant it in the garden. The plant spreads by rhizomes which are sometimes so thick that a saw is needed to cut them.

Potentilla anserina
Silverweed
(Argentine, fair days, silver feather, midsummer silver, prince's feathers.)

Pinnate leaves which are silvery beneath and yellow flowers found from May to August. Spreads by surface runners, rooting at the nodes. An infusion of silverweed was once used against sunburn, to cure sore throats and to check the bleeding of piles.

Silverweed

Polygonum cuspidatum (Reynoutria japonica)
Japanese knotweed
Very tall, large and fast growing, with triangular leaves and a zig-zag stem. It has a branched flowering stem, producing small white flowers from August to October.

Potentilla reptans
Cinquefoil
(Five fingers, 5 leaf grass.)

A creeping weed, often found on alkaline and wet soils. The plant has yellow flowers and stems of up to 1 m, rooting at leaf junctions with 5 leaflets per leaf. Each plant can have a taproot 30 cm long and up to 15 runners. Each runner can grow up to 1 m and have up to 20 nodes. In the following year, each node can produce an individual plant with a 30 cm taproot. In this way the plant can colonise 10 sq m a season!

Cinquefoil

Prunella vulgaris
Self-heal

A lawn weed, particularly widespread on chalky soils, which keeps close to the ground to escape the mower. This plant has a prostrate branching stem, mats of dark green leaves and a mass of dark purple flowers in oblong or square heads, produced from June to November. The plant spreads rapidly with creeping stems that root at the nodes, and also freely reproduces by seed.

Self-heal

As its name suggests, it was once used to cure a variety of ailments from sore throats to wounds. Saint Gerard said of self-heal and bugle, 'In the world there are not two better wound herbs, as hath bin often procured.'

Pteridium aquilinum
Bracken

One of the most common and widespread plants on the planet. It is aggressive, competitive, toxic and carcinogenic. The plant has spread rapidly since the First World War. The fronds grow from 30 to 180 cm, while the spreading underground stems go from 10 to 45 cm deep. The plant has a persistent underground creeping stem, carrying dormant fronds which spring into life when the

Bracken

plant is cut. These underground stems or rhizomes grow 1 m or more a year. As with *Equisetum*, the plant also has two generations, one of which is a sexual phase producing a flimsy tiny green plant. Bracken carries carcinogenic spores and should not be cut when these are being released. It is also toxic to animals and rarely eaten, except in drought and when food is scarce.

However, bracken makes excellent, perfectly safe compost and a good mulch. For this, it is best to cut it when it is young (May) and its potassium content is high.

Ranunculus bulbosus
Bulbous buttercup
(Baffiners, bassinet, bolt, butterdaisy, craw, eggs and butter, gold knobs, St Antony's turnip.)

A short plant with a swollen stem base. The yellow flowers are found from March to June. The plant has no runners but can reproduce from seed and fragments of stem.

The plant is poisonous when green but not when dried as hay. When fresh it inflames and blisters the skin and was once used by beggars to cause open sores in order to get sympathy. It was also rubbed on cows' udders on May Day to increase milk yields.

Ranunculus ficaria
Lesser celandine

A weed of shady places. The plant has fleshy, heart-shaped leaves, bulbils at the base of the leaf stalks, and produces its familiar flowers from March to May. The flowers open at 9 a.m. and

Lesser celandine

close at 5 p.m., also shutting before a shower of rain. Reproduction is by seed and from the bulbils (technically corms).

Medicinally, the plant is called 'pilewort' as the roots resemble haemorrhoids and were once used to treat them! The plant robs the soil of nutrients.

Creeping buttercup

Ranunculus repens
Creeping buttercup

A weed of damp soils. A creeping plant with fleshy white roots and runners. Yellow flowers are produced from May to September.

Seed production is sparse but the plant spreads rapidly by runners that root at the nodes. In this way, one creeping buttercup can spread over 3.5 sq m a year.
(See also illustration on page 9.)

Rubus fruticosus
Bramble

A very variable, scrambling shrub with over 2,000 microspecies, some of which are now sold as cultivated varieties. Has woody, biennial stems and white or pink flowers from May to September which produce one of the most delicious wild foods. The plant spreads by producing roots at the tips of stems and by seeds spread by birds and other animals.

If kept under control, then the plant is an asset in the garden, producing fruit for jam, wine and pies. It is a haven for wildlife and attracts emperor moths, ringlet and gatekeeper butterflies, wasps, flies, spiders and snails. Folklore states that it is unlucky to eat blackberries after 29th September as the devil was said to have spat on them.
(See illustration on page 9.)

21

Sorrel

Rumex acetosa
Sorrel
(Tom thumbs, thousand fingers.)

A weed of light soils. A short or tall, acid-tasting perennial, with arrow-shaped leaves and a head of loose flowers produced from May to August.
The plant has thick underground stems which spread and throw up aerial shoots in clusters. It is also spread by seed.

Rumex acetosella
Sheep's sorrel

Also found on light soils but rarely on lime. A smaller plant with narrow arrow-shaped leaves, which flowers in the same period as *Rumex acetosa*.

Rumex crispus
Curled dock

Tall perennial with narrower leaves than broad-leaved dock, and wavy leaf margins. Flowers from June to October.

Rumex obtusifolius
Broad-leaved dock
(Butterdock, cushy-cows.)

Tall perennial with oblong to lance-shaped leaves. Flowers from June to October. Can indicate an acid, waterlogged soil.
This plant is an excellent survivor. One plant can produce 60,000 seeds a year which are carried far and wide by wind, water and animals. The seeds can remain alive and dormant for fifty years.
Many germinate when the ground is cultivated, generally from March to April and from September to October, and can flower within nine weeks of seedling emergence! The plants soon develop a vertical underground stem and taproot up to 1 m deep and from then on are very difficult to eradicate. If underground parts are cut, then each piece can develop into a new plant. The roots contain a chemical which stops the growth of fungi, other plants and bacteria so there is little competition and the plant will not even rot!
Now for the good news; dock roots act as subsoilers and can retrieve nutrients washed out by the rain. The leaves can be composted to return these foods to the soil. The plant is a purgative and astringent and can relieve nettle stings and other inflammations.

Broad-leaved dock

Sagina procumbens
Pearlwort

A weed of light, dry soils. Often found on worn lawns and paths. A low, tufted plant with prostrate, needle-like side shoots that spread from a central rosette. It is sometimes mistaken for moss. The flowers are very small, often without petals, and are found from May to September. The plant spreads by its creeping, rooting shoots and also by seed which can be carried great distances on the wind.

A close relative is *Sagina apelata*, the annual pearlwort, which is also common on dry, light soils.

Pearlwort

Senecio jacobaea
Ragwort

(Fellon weed, stagger weed, agreen, fiz-gigs, marefart, yack-yard, yellow ellshiners.)

Typical of poor, light soils. A medium/tall biennial or short-lived perennial with pinnate leaves and yellow flower-heads produced in dense flat-topped clusters from July to September. The plant reproduces mainly from seed and can produce between 50,000 and 60,000 fruits which are carried to new sites by the wind. If injured, then ragwort can also reproduce from buds on the roots.

The plant is poisonous to animals and causes cirrhosis of the liver and fatal jaundice. Horses and cows seem to realise this and avoid the plant but sheep are more susceptible. Ragwort is the favourite food of the cinnabar moth caterpillar which accumulates the poison and advertises the fact with its bright yellow and black 'football jersey'. The plant is also kept under control by the ragwort seed-fly; this lays its eggs in the flower-heads and the larvae eat the developing fruits. However, flowers produced late in the season escape the fly.

Ragwort

Comfrey

Symphytum spp.
Comfreys

(Knitbone, boneset, blackwort, gumplant.)

Many types of comfrey grow in Europe. The native comfrey in Britain is wild comfrey (*Symphytum officinale*). This is a tall, stout perennial with broad hairy leaves. The flowers are bell-like, white or mauve, and are found from May to June. The plant produces a deep taproot and new plants grow easily from fragments of root.

Russian comfrey (*Symphytum × uplandicum*) is a natural hybrid between wild comfrey (*Symphytum officinale*) and prickly comfrey (*Symphytum asperum*). It is a semi-sterile hybrid. The plant has purple/blue flowers and is similar to Britain's native comfrey. A range of forms now exist in Britain as a result of crosses with both parents. One of these forms, 'Bocking 14', is commercially available to gardeners for use as a garden fertiliser. Less vigorous, ornamental forms of comfrey also exist, such as *Symphytum grandiflorum* and *Symphytum caucasicum*, and make decorative additions to the herbaceous border. Comfrey, particularly 'Bocking 14', is a true friend to the organic gardener:

● Its taproot can go down 3 m, bringing up subsoil nutrients.

● The plant is an excellent source of potassium, containing two or three times as much as farmyard manure.

● It can be used as a liquid feed, a compost activator, a rapidly decomposing mulch and a source of fertility in potting composts.

23

● It grows rapidly; four to five cuts (each yielding 1.8 to 2.2 kg) can be made per season.

● The plant will keep supplying fertiliser for up to twenty years. Comfrey is mucilaginous and contains allantoin, and has been widely used as a medicinal herb. The mucilage was used to treat intestinal complaints. Allantoin promotes cell division and comfrey ointments are often used to treat wounds.

Tanacetum parthenium
Feverfew
(Devil daisy, nosebleed, headache plant, midwife standby.)

An aromatic, short/medium perennial. An escape which rapidly spreads in gardens and can indicate poor soils. The plant has yellowish, pinnate leaves and produces clusters of daisy-like flowers from June to September. The plant spreads by seed. A useful weed that is disliked by insects. Medicinally, it is used to treat headaches.

Feverfew

Taraxacum spp.
Dandelion
(Bitterwort, blowball, clock, dindle, one o'clocks, pee-a-bed.)

A variable species with many microspecies. Lobed leaves in a rosette. The flower-heads are solitary on hollow, leafless stalks. The plants spread rapidly, using the wind to carry their parachute-like seeds.

The plants are self-fertilising. Dandelions can also regenerate themselves from pieces of root and can still produce shoots if cut off 15 cm below the ground.

Dandelions can be useful:

● The deep taproots bring up subsoil nutrients and the flowers attract hoverflies whose larvae eat aphids.

● The roots can be made into coffee, the flowers into wine, and the leaves, with their high vitamin A and C content, into salads.

● Medicinally, the plant is used as a diuretic and against warts.

● Dandelions produce a gas called ethylene which ripens fruit, e.g. tomatoes.

(See also illustrations on front cover and page 5.)

Trifolium pratense
Red clover

A weed indicating low nitrogen. A low or tall plant which occasionally has a white crescent on the leaflets. The pink or purple flowers are found from May to October. Spreads by seed and is widely cultivated.

Clover attracts bees. Flowers can be used in salads and teas. Medicinally, the plant has been used to treat whooping cough, asthma, cancer and a weak heart.

Red clover

Trifolium repens
White clover

A creeping perennial with rounder leaves than *Trifolium pratense* and white flowers from May to October. Spreads by seed and vegetatively, rooting at leaf junctions.

Tussilago farfara
Coltsfoot

(Clatter clogs, clayt, clayweed, ass's foot, cough-wort, son before the father.)

A weed that indicates a heavy, often waterlogged soil. Short, creeping, downy plant with large heart-shaped leaves. The yellow daisy-like flowers are produced before the leaves, from February to April, on bare stems with purplish scales.

The plant spreads rapidly by creeping underground stems, which regenerate themselves from fragments. Vast quantities of parachute-like seeds can also be seen drifting in the wind in spring. Some of these are used by goldfinches to line their nests.

The plant is important medicinally and infusions of leaves have long been used to treat coughs and lung complaints. In France, chemists sometimes have coltsfoot flowers painted on their shop-fronts to show their profession.

Coltsfoot

Nettle

Urtica dioica
Nettle

(Scaddine, naughty man's plaything.)

A common, extremely useful garden weed indicating fertile ground. A medium/tall plant covered in stinging hairs. Produces green wind-pollinated flowers from June to September. Spreads by its yellow creeping roots and by seed. Nettles have a variety of uses in the garden:

● As a compost activator.

● As a liquid feed and insect repellent.

● As a food. The leaves taste like spinach and can be made into tea or beer.

● Medicinally, as an infusion to treat burns and spots.

● As a food plant for the red admiral, small tortoiseshell butterfly and early greenfly (which boosts the ladybird population).

● The roots were used as flax fibres in the First World War.

Annuals

This section includes annuals, ephemerals and biennials

Aethusa cynapium
Fool's parsley

So named as it looks like parsley but is poisonous. Has long beard-like bracts, an acrid smell, and is hairless with ribbed stems. Flowers from June to October. One plant can produce up to 6,000 fruits. The leaves contain coniine, like the active poison in hemlock. The plant is not thought to be poisonous when dry.

Fool's parsley

Agrostemma githago
Corn cockle

(Corn campion, drawk, wild savager.)

A tall, erect plant with hairy, long narrow leaves and dark pink flowers from May to August. One plant produces 20 to 40 seeds which used to ripen with the corn.

The seeds are very poisonous and, due to this, the plant has almost been eradicated. It is now often prized as a garden flower. In the sixteenth

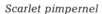
Corn cockle

century the seeds used to contaminate rye and wheat, and those who ate the bread were thought to be prone to leprosy.

Anagallis arvensis
Scarlet pimpernel

(Poor man's weather-glass, bird's eye, shepherd's calendar, wink-a-peep.)

Prostrate plant with square stems and pointed oval leaves in pairs. Flowers found from May to

Scarlet pimpernel

October, usually pale scarlet but sometimes pink, lilac or blue. The flowers open when fine and shut when rain is forecast. Found on light soils.

Borage

Borago officinalis
Borage

A hairy annual with cucumber-scented juice. Bright blue flowers are borne from May to September.

A native of the Mediterranean, this plant (which colonises disturbed ground) has become a 'weed' in Britain. The flowers can be used in drinks to make them cool and refreshing, or crystallised in sugar to use as cake decorations. The plant was sometimes used medicinally to drive away melancholy.

Capsella bursa-pastoris
Shepherd's purse
(Bad man's oatmeal, pepper and salt, pick-pocket, toothwort.)

An ephemeral, cruciferous weed. A variable, low/medium plant. The leaves can be toothed or untoothed. The white flowers are found all the year round, and form heart-shaped seed-pods filled with yellow flat seeds, hence the common name.

The plant often overwinters as a rosette, flowering in the spring. Although visited by insects, the flowers self-pollinate before they open. The plant contains vitamin K, and was used to stop bleeding as well as being a diuretic. It is host for white blister rust which can also affect brassicas.

Shepherd's purse

Cardamine flexuosa, Cardamine hirsuta
Wavy and hairy bittercress
(Jumping cress.)

Common ephemeral weeds. Low/short, hairy plants with a rosette of pinnate leaves resembling small watercress leaves. The tiny white flowers are found from February to November.

The plants produce seeds whenever the weather is not too cold. The seed-pods are explosive, shedding the seeds 80 cm from the plant in all directions when touched or when the pods are ripe. When wet the seeds become sticky, sticking to boots and tools, spreading them even further.

Wavy bittercress

27

Cerastium glomeratum
Sticky mouse-ear

Low, stickily hairy, yellowish annual. The small flowers rarely open, and self-pollinate. The plant usually germinates in autumn and flowers in the spring. Found mainly on dry, sandy soils.

Sticky mouse-ear

Chenopodium album
Fat hen

(Biacon weed, drought-weed, lamb's tongue, frost-blite, wild spinach, pigweed.)

Medium/tall plant. The dark green leaves are covered with a mealy white coat. The plant flowers from June to October. Fat hen produces two types of seed; the soft type can germinate straight away and the hard type can remain dormant in the soil for up to thirty years.

The plant indicates fertile soil and sometimes has a red tinge if the soil is low in phosphate.

Fat hen was once eaten as a vegetable. It contains more iron, calcium, protein and vitamin B than cabbage. However, like rhubarb leaves, the plant contains oxalic acid which locks up iron and calcium and makes them indigestible.

Fat hen

Euphorbia helioscopia
Sun spurge

(Cat's milk, devil's milk, milkwort, Saturday's milk.)

A common weed, often on heavy, limy soil. A short, hairless plant with oval leaves. The flowers, found between April and November, are tiny with no petals and have large greenish/yellow bracts. The seeds shoot out when ripe and are also spread by ants. The plant gives out a milky fluid which is an irritant but was used to cure warts. The nectar attracts many insects.

Sun spurge

Euphorbia lathyrus
Caper spurge

A handsome, striking plant. The thin leaves jut out from the stem horizontally, at right angles to each other. *Euphorbia lathyrus* is a biennial and, in its second year, produces puffy caper-like fruits which are poisonous.

Euphorbia peplus
Petty spurge

A short, hairless plant with tiny green flowers.

Petty spurge

Fumaria officinalis
Fumitory

(Beggary, wax dolls, God's fingers and thumbs.)

A common weed on light soils, especially in the east of Britain.The bright red stem goes brown as the leaves develop. Greyish carrot-like leaves. Pink flowers with dark pink tips, found from April to October. The seeds can remain dormant for some time, but some germinate each spring and can make large spreading plants in moist, fertile soil.

Fumitory was often used medicinally as a tonic, mild aperient and against scurvy. In the Middle Ages it was known as *fumus terrae* (smoke of the earth) as the plant looked as if it was seeping out of the ground like smoke.

Galium aparine
Goosegrass

(Cleavers, Clir up, beggar weed, bleedy tongues, cling, rascal, willy run hedge, sticky willie, stick a back, gentleman's tormentors.)

A very well-known scrambling, sticking weed. The long thin leaves occur in whorls. The plant is covered with down-turned prickles which stick to passers-by. The plant scrambles over other plants forming a dense mat. The dull white flowers are found from May to September. The seeds, sometimes known as 'sweethearts', are spread by sticking to animals.

Geese like to eat this plant and it used to be chopped up in milk to make a tonic to strengthen the hair and teeth. The roots give a red dye.

Goosegrass

Herb Robert

Geranium robertianum
Herb Robert

A weed that flourishes in unkempt conditions and is the most common geranium in Britain. A strong smelling annual, often with a reddish tinge. The pink flowers are found from April to November. Found in shady places.

Geranium spp.
Cranesbills

Geranium molle is a common weed of sandy soils. It is semi-prostrate and has hairy stems. The flowers are pinky purple and found from April to September. They are smaller than those of herb Robert. Another cranesbill that sometimes occurs as a weed is *Geranium dissectum*, the cut-foot cranesbill. This has an upright stem and more finely divided leaves than the other species. The plant was once used medicinally to treat piles and internal bleeding. The perennial *Geranium sanguineum* (bloody cranesbill) is another close relative, which can be distinguished by its striking solitary crimson flowers.

Bloody cranesbill

29

Impatiens glandulifera
Himalayan balsam
(Policeman's helmet.)

A garden escape, brought to Britain from India in the colonial days. A tall plant with reddish hollow stems, and simple green leaves with small red 'teeth' at the margins. Sweet smelling. The pink flowers are borne from July to October. The seed-pods are explosive and, when ripe, release seeds when touched or shaken. The plant thrives in damp soils.

Himalayan balsam

Lamium purpureum
Red dead-nettle
(Badman's posies, rabbit meat, day nettle.)

A member of the mint family. A low/short, downy, aromatic annual with pink flowers. The plant can flower and seed all year round if the weather conditions allow, and the plants often set seed when you are preparing your seedbeds. The seeds are distributed by ants.

Red dead-nettle

Nipplewort

Lapsana communis
Nipplewort

A common weed on heavier soils. A short or tall annual with toothed, pointed oval leaves. Has clusters of dandelion-like flowers which do not open in dull weather.

Unlike many other members of the family, nipplewort does not exude a milky juice. The flowers and seeds are produced from June to October. An average-sized plant can produce up to 1,000 fruits. Nipplewort is a relative of lettuce and can be eaten in salads although it is quite bitter.

Its name is thought to be derived from the herbals of the fourteenth century when it was used to heal ulcers of the nipples!

Pineapple mayweed

Matricaria matricariodes (Chamomilla suaveolens)
Pineapple mayweed
(Rayless mayweed.)

An annual found on compacted pathways. A low/short plant with feathery leaves and a strong smell of pineapple. The flower-heads are egg shaped, yellow/green without petals and are found from May to November.

About 7,000 fruits are produced per plant and these are spread by rainwater, and in mud on the feet and vehicles.

Medicago spp.
Medicks

There are many species of medick, often found as lawn weeds or on coastal soils. Two common medicks that occur as weeds are *Medicago arabica* (spotted medick) and *Medicago lupulina* (black medick). Both are legumes, but their seed-pods are atypical being curved or coiled.

Black medick is a downy, prostrate plant with clover-like leaves. The yellow flowers also resemble clover. They are found from April to October and produce black seed-pods.

Spotted medick, as its name suggests, has a black spot on its leaflets. The yellow flower-heads contain less flowers (one to four) than black medick and the seed-pods are spiny and coiled.

Medick

Forget-me-not

Mercurialis annua
Annual dog's mercury

A late summer annual found on light, sandy soils, especially in London gardens. The plant is rare or absent in the north of Britain.

Mercurialis annua is similar to its perennial relative, *Mercurialis perennis*, but is paler, hairless and sometimes branched. The plant needs warmth to flower and flowers are usually found from late May to November. In good conditions the plant can complete its life cycle in twelve weeks and spreads by using explosive seed-pods. Annual dog's mercury is poisonous and if eaten, then can cause symptoms like gastroenteritis.

Myosotis arvensis
Forget-me-not

(Bird's eye, blue mouse-ear, scorpion grass.)

One of many *myosotis* species. A short, hairy annual (or biennial). Rosettes of leaves send up flowering stalks. The small, delicate pale grey/blue flowers are borne from April to October. The

seeds become gluey when wet and are easily spread by attaching to passers-by. Many seeds remain dormant but some germinate every autumn and overwinter as a rosette.

Oxalis corniculata
Oxalis

A short, creeping annual (or perennial) which roots at leaf junctions with shamrock-type leaves. The bright yellow flowers are found from May to October. The plant is not native to Britain and arrived in foreign seed. The plant spreads by shooting seeds out of its exploding pods. Several other species of Oxalis from the Southern Hemisphere have recently become pests in British gardens.

Oxalis

Papaver spp.

Poppies

(Blind eyes, poppet, redweed, sleepyhead.)

The wild red poppy (*Papaver rhoeas*) was once a well-known sight in cornfields and occasionally pops up from dormant seeds as a garden weed. A medium plant with hairy leaves and stems, and dark red flowers with dark centres and blue/black anthers (producing pollen). The pods are round and hairless. Four other species of field poppy, *Papaver dubium, Papaver leoqii, Papaver hybridum, Papaver argemone*, are distinguished by their seed-pods. The seeds can remain dormant for many years. Poppies are used in Britain on Remembrance Day because they sprang up when the trenches were dug in the First World War and the seeds were exposed to the surface.

Opium poppy

Poppy

colouring inks. The plant produces no nectar but is valued by insects for its pollen.

Another species, *Papaver somniferum* (the opium poppy) with its pale green/grey leaves and pink, mauve and white flowers has now become a widespread garden escape.

Poa annua

Annual meadow-grass

(Causeway grass, Suffolk grass.)

A common weed on all soils except chalk. A short grass, yellow green, sometimes with purple spikelets. It has no awns and no underground shoots. The plant varies greatly in size depending on the availability of water and nutrients. The plant can flower and germinate at any time of the year, especially in the spring.

Annual meadow-grass

The species were thought to be slightly narcotic and many parts of the plant have been used medicinally. Leaves were made into tea, an infusion of the petals was used to cure throat infections and coughs, and seeds aided pain relief. A syrup from the plant was once used as a dye for

Knotgrass

Polygonum aviculare
Knotgrass

(Allseed, armstrong, cow grass, ninety knot, redlegs, surface twitch, wireweed.)

Often regarded as one of the most difficult annual weeds to eradicate. A common species, especially on sandy soils.

A low, hairless plant with larger leaves on the main stem than on the branches. Sleeve-like, transparent, papery upgrowths (ochreae) are found arising from the leaf bases encircling the stem. Small pink and white flowers are found at the base of the upper leaves from June to November.

Knotgrass spreads by seeds, some of which remain dormant for many years. However, it does have other survival tactics. The plant matures and spreads rapidly, its wiry shoots easily extending over 0.2 sq m. Like perennials, knotgrass sends down a taproot that can reach depths of 30 to 60 cm in sandy soils. The plant is very difficult to hoe out and can regenerate itself if the top is cut off during the growing season.

Redshank

Polygonum persicaria
Redshank

(Red spot, persicaria, crabgrass, lakeweed, saucy Alice, peachwort, Virgin Mary's pinch.)

Occurs on moist soil. A medium, sprawling, hairless, branched annual with dark 'arrowhead' spots on the leaves. The pink flowers occur in densely crowded spikes from June to October.

The seeds of redshank are edible and have been found in the stomach of early Iron Age man.

Scandix pecten-veneris
Shepherd's needle

(Adam's needle, crakeneedle, elshins, old wives' darning needles.)

This once common weed is now almost extinct due to the use of weedkillers. It is occasionally found on chalklands.

A short annual with carrot-like leaves being a member of the umbellifer family. The plant has simple white umbels of flowers from May to August. Its main distinguishing feature, from which it gets its common name, comes from the conspicuous needle-like fruits, which can be up to 8 cm long! The seed-pods are covered in fine up-pointing spines which help the seed bury itself in the soil.

Shepherd's needle

Senecio vulgaris
Groundsel

(Birdseed, grinning swallow, switchen.)

A very common ephemeral, especially on damp, heavy soils. A short plant with thin 'oak-like' leaves. Groundsel has 'rayless' yellow flower-heads which can occur at any time of year. The seeds are carried long distances on their parachutes by the wind, and can germinate, grow and set seed in five weeks.

The plant was once used as a purgative, diuretic and poultice for ulcers. A sniff of the fresh roots was said to cure headaches and the leaves were steeped in milk and given to children when teething. The entire plant is a food source of the cinnabar moth caterpillar (see ragwort, page 23) and the seeds are eaten by goldfinches and linnets.

Charlock

Groundsel

Sinapis arvensis
Charlock
(Birdseed, kinkle, bastard rocket, redlock, willkail.)

An agricultural weed that can easily be introduced into gardens on manure and in chicken feed. A medium/tall, hairy plant of the cabbage family. The lower leaves are larger than the upper leaves, have no stalks and do not clasp the stems. The yellow flowers, found from April to October, produce radish-like pods. Charlock can carry many of the pests and diseases that affect

cabbages, such as club root, flea beetle, and turnip downy mildew.

The green manure, white mustard, can also become a weed if left to seed. It can be distinguished from charlock by its larger yellow flowers and more regularly lobed leaves.

Sisymbrium officinale
Hedge mustard
(Winy jack, singer's plant.)

A member of the cabbage family and a common wayside weed. A medium tall, stiff annual with spreading branches and a 'candelabra' growth habit. From May to September, small yellow flowers are found at the top of the stem above the short vertical seed-pods pressed against the stem. The seeds can germinate in the autumn or spring. Hedge mustard carries many of the pests and diseases that affect brassicas.

An infusion of the plant was used in former days for throat diseases and was considered, in the time of Louis XIV, an excellent remedy for the loss of the voice.

Sonchus asper
Prickly sowthistle

An annual sowthistle which can be distinguished from *Sonchus oleraceus* as its leaves are less lobed with sharper spines and clasp the stem firmly with rounded lobes.

34

Prickly sowthistle

A short, stickily hairy annual with very characteristic needle-like leaves in whorls. Tiny white flowers are found from May to September.

The seeds can germinate in autumn and spring. In suitable weather conditions the plant can complete its life cycle in eight weeks. A close relative, *Spergula sativa*, was cultivated for its seeds, used in cattle and chicken fodder.

Stellaria media
Chickweed
(Hen's inheritance, maruns, chuckenwort.)

A very common ephemeral weed. A prostrate plant with oval leaves, the lower ones being stalked. The tiny white flowers have petals split to the base and occur all the year round.

This plant is very 'maternal', folding its leaves over the buds at night to protect them. The flowers only live for one day, but there are many of them. Each plant can produce 2,000 seeds, each of which can complete its life cycle in seven weeks!

The plant indicates fertile soil and is edible. It is rich in the minerals needed in your diet. Chickweed water was an old wives' remedy for obesity.

Chickweed

Sonchus oleraceus
Smooth sowthistle
(Milkweed, dindle, milky dickles, hare's lettuce.)

A short or tall, greyish, hairless annual. The lobed leaves have softly spiny margins and clasp the stem with arrow-shaped points. Like many perennials, the plant has a deep, tough taproot and is difficult to pull up.

Dandelion-like flowers are produced in a cluster from May to November. About 6,000 seeds are produced per plant, and are spread by the wind. If the plant is cut and buried when in flower, then the seeds will mature and germinate when brought to the surface again.

Smooth sowthistle indicates fertile soils. It makes an excellent rabbit food, but, unfortunately, is also a host to the lettuce root aphid.

Spergula arvensis
Corn spurrey
(Beggar weed, bottle brush, dother, mountain flax, pick purse, poverty weed.)

A common weed on acid and sandy soils, surviving at pH 4.0!

Corn spurrey

Tragopogon pratensis
Goatsbeard
(Jack-go-to-bed-at-noon, noon flower.)

A medium, hairless annual (or perennial!) with grass-like leaves. The dandelion-like flowers are shorter than the green sepals around them, and only open on sunny mornings (from May to August). The seed-heads look like large, delicate dandelion clocks.

The tapering roots were once eaten like parsnips and the stems cut and boiled like asparagus.

35

Scentless mayweed

Tripleurospermum inodorum (Matricaria perforata)
Scentless mayweed
(White gowlan, dog's chamomile.)

A short, half-prostrate annual with no scent and feathery leaves. The common name 'dog' chamomile means the plant is inferior to chamomile.

The daisy-like flowers are found from April to October. Like pineapple mayweed, a close relative, the plant colonises compacted paths and walkways.

Veronica spp.
Speedwells

There are many species of *Veronica* found in the garden.

Veronica persica
Common field speedwell

An import, arriving in Britain in 1825. A low, sprawling annual with pointed lobes on the

Germander speedwell

leaves. The sky blue flowers are self-fertilising. They have dark veins and a white lower petal, and occur from March to May. The plants creep up and root from the stem. They also spread by seed (up to 6,000 a plant) and are dispersed by ants and man.

Another import into Britain is *Veronica filiformis* (slender speedwell). This was introduced from Caucasus as a rock-garden plant and is now a common lawn weed. A low, sprawling perennial with bluntly oval, kidney-shaped leaves. The bright blue flowers have a purple tinge and are found from April to June.

Veronica chamaedrys (germander speedwell) is another low, sprawling perennial with oval pointed leaves. The flowers are bright blue with a white eye and occur from April to June. The plant was used as a blood purifier and to treat lung complaints.

Vicia spp.
Vetches

Many vetches occasionally occur as weeds in gardens, but they were once a serious problem in cornfields, clambering over and smothering the crop.

Vicia hirsuta
Hairy vetch

A short, slender annual with fern-like leaves and unbranched tendrils at the tips of the leaves. Pale lilac flowers occur in a spike from May to August. A close relative is *Vicia cracca* (tufted vetch) which in contrast is tall, scrambling and perennial.

Tufted vetch

Vicia tetrasperma
Smooth tare

This vetch is similar to *Vicia hirsuta* but has larger flowers and hairless pods.

Smooth tare

Viola spp.
Pansy

A beautiful plant that hybridizes readily. Two of the annuals that are fairly common in gardens are *Viola arvensis* and *Viola tricolor*.

Viola arvensis
Field pansy

A variable, low annual. The lower leaves are stalked and oval, and the upper leaves thinner. The flowers are cream coloured, sometimes tinged with violet or yellow, and occur from April to November.

Viola tricolor
Wild pansy
(Beedy eyes, call me to you, heartscone, meet-her-i'-th'-entry-kiss-her-i'-th'-buttery, idle.)

A variable, low annual. The lower leaves are stalked and oval to lanceolate. The flowers, occurring from April to November, are violet, yellow, or both. In wet weather the flower-heads droop to protect them from the rain. Seeds are shed from the pods throughout the summer.
Medicinally, the plant was reputed as a remedy for epilepsy, asthma, sickness and numerous other complaints. The flowers were used for heart disease, and it is this, as well as the belief that an infusion worked as a love potion, that gave the plant its common name. The dried leaves were used as a remedy for 'cradle cap' in children. On the continent, pansy leaves are used in place of litmus paper in acid and alkali tests.

Wild pansy

The benefits of weeds

Many gardeners pull up 'wild flowers' from their gardens because they are known 'weeds' or just because they have not been planted. However, weeds are not all bad.

If you see a 'weed' in your garden, then stop to think before you remove it. Is it really competing with your vegetables or ornamentals, and, if not, then does it have any attributes? Many 'weeds' are attractive, free wild flowers, and are also beneficial to wildlife and the soil. Even if the weeds are competing or causing a problem, they have many uses when they are pulled up. They can be put on the compost or used as a tasty addition to your diet.

Organic gardeners tolerate some weeds, and make the best use of them both in and out of the ground. After all, if you did not cultivate the ground, then the weeds would not be there in the first place.

Benefits of weeds whilst growing

Weed examples	Benefits	
Chickweed, clover, vetch.	● Can act as a green manure:	Provide ground cover. Protect soil surface from heavy rain. Encourage soil life. Dig the soil with their roots. Prevent leaching of nutrients. Increase fertility. Control erosion. Improve microclimate.
Corn cockle increases the yield of wheat, nettles enhance the flavour of herbs.	● Contain beneficial chemicals:	To enhance the growth of other plants.
All weeds.	● Increase diversity:	Fewer pests. Tap the soil for different nutrients.
Dock, dandelion, comfrey.	● Act as subsoilers:	Bring up nutrients from the subsoil. Improve structure and drainage of soil.
See page 41.	● Act as indicators:	Different weeds grow on different types of soils.
Knotgrass, hedge bindweed, dandelion, poppy, teasel, thistle, chickweed, shepherd's purse, plantain.	● Are a food source for a range of wildlife:	Birds: seed.
Field bindweed, bramble, thistle, ivy, dandelion, campion, medick, groundsel.		Butterflies: nectar.
Thistle, fat hen, medick, ivy, campion, groundsel, clover, white dead-nettle.		Bees: nectar.
Campion.		Moths: nectar.
Dock, sorrel, nettle, groundsel, ragwort, burdock, charlock, bindweed.		Caterpillars: foliage.
Sun spurge, fumitory.		Ants: seed oils.
Nettle, fat hen, medick, dandelion, nipplewort, bindweed.		Predators: attract ladybirds and hoverflies whose larvae eat aphids.
Creeping thistle, ground elder, nettle, shepherd's purse, chickweed.		Beetles.
Ivy.	● Provide shelter:	Cover for birds. Hibernation for butterflies.
Daisy, toadflax, red dead-nettle, campion, comfrey, poppy.	● Are attractive:	Flowers provide colour in the garden

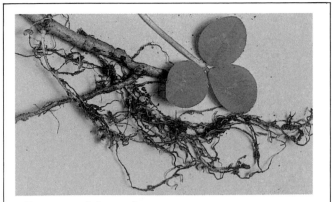

Nitrogen nodule on clover

Hoverfly

Finch

Benefits of weeds once 'harvested'

Many weeds, or parts of weeds, are useful when they have been 'harvested', so never burn them or put them out with the rubbish.

Weeds and compost are inseparable, and weeds are often the only plants added whole to the heap. Their explorative roots take up vital nutrients, including the all-important trace elements. Some weeds may be rich in one particular element, e.g. iron in nettles, while others may contain only a trace, but, whatever the quantity, all the nutrients have been taken from the soil and must be returned, either by hoeing and allowing them to decay on the ground or by adding them to the heap.

Some particularly useful additions to the heap include:

● Chamomile – rich in iron, calcium, phosphate, sulphur.

● Yarrow – rich in iron, calcium, potash, phosphate, nitrogen, sulphur.

● Stinging nettle – rich in iron, nitrogen.

● Dandelion – rich in iron, sodium, potash, phosphate.

● Comfrey – rich in nitrogen and potash.

These plants, with a few other ingredients, make up the basis of some herbal compost activators. So 'weeding' is not all drudgery; you are, in fact, gathering nutrients and organic matter.

Nettle and comfrey liquids also make excellent liquid feeds. Horsetail contains large quantities of silica and some find that a foliar spray from an infusion of this weed helps to protect plants from fungal attack, especially mildew.

Weeds can also be used as herbs, medicines, salads, spices, vegetables, beverages, dyes and even textiles! Young leaves of many weeds can be eaten in salads. These include hairy bittercress, white mustard, hedge garlic, parsley piert, salad burnet, dandelion, nipplewort, cat's-ear and goatsbeard. Some can be cooked like spinach and served with butter or in flans or soups. Ground elder was introduced into Britain as a vegetable, but chickweed, shepherd's purse, rosebay willowherb,

39

red and white dead-nettles, charlock and goosegrass are amongst the weeds which could also end up on the plate. Fat hen is often recommended as a green vegetable but contains a large amount of oxalic acid and can be poisonous if eaten in large quantities.

Leaves are not the only edible portions. Stems of yarrow, hogweed, goatsbeard and burdock can be eaten like asparagus, after removing the hard outer tissue. Burdock stems have a crisp, nutty, fennel/cucumber flavour. In the past, children used to chew the scrubbed roots of restharrow like liquorice. Silverweed roots, too, have culinary value and can be baked or boiled like potatoes. Dandelion roots can be scrubbed, dried and ground as a coffee substitute.

Dandelion wine

Pour 4.5 litres of boiling water over 10 handfuls of freshly picked flowers. Cover and stand. After three days, strain the mixture, boil the liquid for thirty minutes and then add 1.5 kg of sugar, some grated ginger root and the rind of a lemon and an orange. When cool, add yeast to ferment and cover for two days. Finally, decant into demijohns and store until ready.

Nettle beer

Ingredients:
9 litres cold water
1 bucketful washed nettle tops
4 handfuls dandelion flowers
4 handfuls goosegrass
56 g ginger

Boil all the ingredients for forty minutes, then strain and discard the plant material (on the compost heap). Add 2 cupfuls of brown sugar and 28 g yeast to the liquid and stand in a warm place for seven hours. Then, remove any scum, add 1 tablespoon of tartar, bottle and cork securely. When ready, this pleasant drink is rather reminiscent of ginger beer and was once used as a remedy for rheumatic pains.

Sorrel soup *Rumex acetosa*

Chop 50 g sorrel leaves with a large onion and a sprig of rosemary. Mix with a tablespoon of flour, and simmer in 85 g butter for ten minutes, stirring continuously. Add 2 litres of boiling water, 2 tablespoons of breadcrumbs and seasoning. Simmer for one hour. Just before serving, stir in a well-beaten mixture of 2 egg yolks and 150 ml cream.

Sorrel Sauce

Sorrel can be pulped raw and mixed with sugar and vinegar to make a pleasant sauce which goes well with fish dishes.

Nettle pudding

A Scottish recipe for a tasty savoury dish.
Ingredients:
4.5 litres young nettle tops
2 leeks (chopped)
2 heads broccoli (chopped)
110 g rice (parboiled)

Place all ingredients in a muslin bag, tie tightly and boil for thirty minutes. Strain, untie and serve with gravy.

Many weeds which are too strong to eat in large quantities can be used as herbs. Cow parsley can be used to flavour herb omelettes, but take care not to use hemlock or fool's parsley as these are both poisonous. Borage petals make a fragrant, attractive addition to claret cups, and can be chewed or infused in hot water the next morning for hangovers! Seeds of the field poppy are not narcotic and can be used to decorate bread, rolls and cakes (before baking). Also, try adding them to honey as a dressing for fruit; very tasty.

The medicinal qualities of many weeds have been known for some time. Many of these plants were prescribed as cures just because they resembled the illness or affliction. This is known as 'the doctrine of signatures.' For example, lesser celandine is also known as 'pilewort' and the bulbous roots were used to treat haemorrhoids! Recent medical research has shown that many weeds are useful. Feverfew contains sesquiterpine and acetones which can reduce migraines. Many sufferers eat the chopped leaves in sandwiches.

'Even when we don't eat 'em we can still

beat 'em.' Nettles have been used by the textile industry in Europe. They are stronger than flax and less harsh than hemp. They also yield a green dye which was used in the Second World War on camouflage nets. Goosegrass seeds have also had their heyday and were used to adorn the top of lacemakers' pins to make a sort of padded head.

Weeds as soil indicators

Weed communities tend to prefer different types of soil and can, therefore, be used as soil indicators, showing whether the soil is wet, dry, acid or alkaline. If you cultivate your garden, or add manures or liming materials, then it will obviously change the weeds that you find.

If you are taking on a new garden, or making a start on an old one, then look at the weeds before you start work. This table shows you what soil types you may have.

Chickweed is an all-round indicator of fertile, well-structured soil, so do not despair if you see it in your garden. A final thought. Some of the 'weeds' in your garden are now becoming very rare. One of these is shepherd's needle. So, when you cultivate or 'improve' your soil, leave a small sanctuary for the native flora.

Indicator weeds

Weeds	Indicate	Comment
Field pansy, field mouse-ear, poppy, charlock.	Calcareous soil.	Test pH. No liming required. Acid-loving plants will need to be planted in acid compost.
Corn spurrey, sorrel, plantain, parsley piert.	Low pH (acidic).	Test pH. May require liming.
Chickweed.	Neutral soil.	Just right!
Cleavers, red dead-nettle, chickweed, borage, creeping thistle, sun spurge, fumitory, charlock, speedwell, redshank.	High in nutrients.	Use organic matter to maintain fertility.
Groundsel, stinging nettle, fat hen, ground elder, dock, sowthistle, chickweed.	High nitrogen.	Plants may be sappy. Leafy vegetables will thrive. Shrubs, perennials and annuals may flower less. Balance nutrients (with seaweed compost).
Increase in weeds that flower in summer/autumn.	Declining fertility/neglect.	Add organic matter. Sow green manures. Recycle nutrients. Maintain ground cover.
Clover, medick, vetch.	Low nitrogen.	Grow nitrogen-fixing green manures (tares, clover).
Silverweed, greater plantain, pineapple mayweed.	Compact soil.	Sow green manures. Make deep beds. Cover soil. Add organic matter. Double dig.
Creeping buttercup, horsetail, silverweed, coltsfoot.	Poor drainage.	Aerate soil. Make deep beds. Sow green manures. Add organic matter. Double dig.
Speedwell, fumitory, chickweed.	Well-aerated, moist soils.	Just right!
Spurges, chickweed, groundsel, fat hen, dandelion.	High in humus.	Just right!

Problems with weeds

Although weeds do have many benefits, they are very aggressive and if left to their own devices, then they would soon take the place of the plants that you want to grow. Many weeds:

- Can compete with your cultivated plants for light, water and nutrients.
- Are poisonous.
- Can 'attack' or spoil your crops.
- Can make harvesting difficult.
- May look unsightly in certain situations.
- Can spread pests and diseases.

Competition

Onion crops can suffer badly if they are not weeded. In the first couple of weeks after germinating the seedlings benefit from a 'nurse' crop of weeds. After this the onions desperately need light to give them energy to feed the growing bulbs. They have thin, strap-like leaves which can easily be shaded out by weeds. If their competitors are not removed, then the potential yield of the onion bulbs can drop by up to 4% a day. Do not leave it too late either, as they do not recover from an early setback. Other plants, such as marrows and potatoes, fight back and smother out weeds, giving as good as they get.

Competition also takes place underground, particularly from the perennial weeds. Horsetail is an example; its thin leaves cast little shade, but the tenacious roots greedily rob the soil of nutrients.

The ability of weeds to compete also depends on the season. Chickweed that germinates in the summer is not usually a problem and can even act as a 'green manure' under maturing plants. In the spring it is a different story, and chickweed can be a real menace in areas such as the seedbed.

Attacking or spoiling crops

Bindweed can become a real headache in beds that are permanently planted with fruit or ornamentals. It uses these plants to climb up to the sun, strangling and shading as it goes. Couch grass, too, can be particularly vicious, as those of you who have used potatoes to shade it out will probably have found. It impails the offending potato tubers with its strong, sharp rhizomes, grows right through them and keeps on going. As well as attacking crops, some weeds such as ivy can also damage walls if they are in a bad state of repair.

Ivy invading a house

Poisonous weeds

Ragwort and corn cockle are poisonous, so keep them well away from pets and children. If corn cockles are grown in the flower-beds, then make sure that the flower-heads are removed as they go over, as it is the seeds that contain the toxins.

Harvesting

This is far less of a problem in the garden than on the farm where machinery is used. The main problem arises from the weeds which resemble the crop and go unnoticed, and also from the ones that fight back. Small nettles often lurk unseen in strawberry beds and are only painfully discovered when harvesting, by which time the roots are well entwined with those of the strawberries.

Unsightly weeds

Many gardeners like tidy, formal gardens. In these situations, any plant spoiling the appearance of plants in plots, borders, paths or lawns would be removed even though there is little or no competition.

Pests and diseases

Pests and diseases are commonly harboured on weeds and many common ones are listed in the table.

Some weed pests can actually be beneficial. Host-specific aphids found early in the season on nettles provide a spring meal for ladybirds. This may increase the numbers of this predator which can then move onto the flowers and vegetables, picking off the aphids here before they become a problem. At the other extreme come the cutworms, pests which attack roots and stems. If a weedy patch is cultivated and their food source removed, then they will happily move onto the crop plants.

Diseases cause more of a problem. Many cruciferous weeds, e.g. charlock and shepherd's purse, transmit the fungal disease club root whether dead or alive. So, if you are rotating carefully to get rid of this disease, then make sure that you remove the crucifers too. Shepherd's purse also carries the disease white rust (which can spread to brassicas) but, fortunately, not the pest cabbage root fly.

Many weeds act as hosts for viral diseases. The viruses are spread from 'weed' to 'crop' by sap-sucking insects such as aphids, as they travel from plant to plant. Although the virus may cause death of the crop, it can go unnoticed in its 'weed' host. Ornamentals, too, act as viral hosts, e.g. wallflower can carry turnip mosaic virus.

Weed	Pest/disease	Crop affected
Chickweed.	Red spider mite, whitefly.	Glasshouse crops.
Fat hen, dock.	Aphid.	Broad beans.
Sowthistle.	Leaf miner.	Chrysanthemums.
Speedwell.	Stem/bulb nematode.	Bulbs (e.g. daffodil).
Groundsel.	Rust.	Cinerarias.
Chickweed, groundsel.	Cucumber mosaic virus.	Marrows, tomatoes.
Shepherd's purse, groundsel, fat hen, hairy bittercress.	Beet western yellows (virus).	Lettuce (outer leaves turn yellow).
Shepherd's purse and other crucifers.	Cauliflower mosaic viruses.	Brassicas.

Red spider mite on melon

For further details on viral diseases in plants refer to the companion volume in this series, *Healthy Fruit and Vegetables: How to avoid diseases, disorders and deficiencies* by Pauline Pears and Bob Sherman.

Principles of organic weed control

The main aim of organic weed control is to remove weeds to a level where no competition arises. Weedkillers may seem like an easy option but *there is no such thing as an organic weedkiller*. Weedkillers do not only kill weeds but have far-reaching effects on the environment, including wildlife, soil organisms, people and pets. Scientific data has shown that some may be irritants (2.4.D, aminotriazole, dalapon, MCPA, dicamba), some can affect fish and other animals, (glyphosphate) and some are even suspected of causing cancer (2.4.D, aminotriazole). In one research station it was noted that a plot regularly treated with paraquat and diquat contained no earthworms and had a significant reduction in other soil life. Paraquat is also known to be toxic to mammals and can cause permanent damage to internal organs.

In the garden, a place of recreation and pleasure, it is unnecessary to resort to weedkillers, even though herbicide formulations for amateur use are very dilute and have safety precautions well marked on the labels. Organic methods are just as effective and no more time-consuming in the long run. There are many ways of controlling weeds organically, both preventative and curative. The method that you use will depend on the weeds present, the area in which they are to be controlled, such as on a path or in a permanent or annual bed, time and financial constraints. The table outlines some of the general methods that you may like to try. Further details are given on the following pages. Whichever method you choose, there are three principles to remember:

● Weeds are green plants. Plants need light. Therefore, no light, no weeds!

● Keep on top of your weeds. Remove them as soon as you see them (if they are likely to become a problem).

● Do not let them flower and seed. The saying 'one year seeding, seven years weeding' is as true today as it ever was. It is best to remove weed flowers even before they have opened as many weeds can seed when the plant has been pulled up!

Weed control

Method	Comment
Good composting	● Peak heating compost ● Dealing with perennial roots.
Presowing cultivations	● Stale seedbed technique. ● Rotovating, double digging. ● Removing the surface cover.
Plant raising	● In modules. ● Healthy plant, faster growth.
Mulching	● To exclude light. ● Which mulch for which job?
Green manures	● Weed-suppressing varieties.
Raised beds	● No dig, no weed.
Rotation	● A design to keep weeds at bay.
Hygiene	● Fences and moats.
Hoeing	● Appropriate tools and times.
Flame weeding	● Tools and techniques.
New ideas	● Biological control.

Compost

Weeds are some of the few plants returned whole to the compost heap. They are a real asset as they contain the correct balance of nutrients for healthy plant growth.

It is possible to destroy weed seeds by composting, but it is important to get the compost hot enough or some may survive to give a real problem when the composted material is spread.

The companion volume in this series, *How to make your Garden Fertile* by Pauline Pears, gives full details on the composting process, but here are a few hints to make sure that you really cook those weeds.

Getting it hot

1. The container should be at least 120 sq cm.
2. The box should have solid sides to retain heat.
3. Make sure air can get in through base.
4. Build a heap all in one go.
5. Use a wide variety of ingredients, including some rich in nitrogen, to enable the micro-organisms to work up a heat.
6. Chop the ingredients up well, and mix to get quicker heating.
7. The heap should be just moist enough to drip a couple of drops of water when a handful is squeezed hard.
8. Do not add lumps of soil as this can make it cold.
9. Cover the compost with a carpet to keep in the warmth.
10. Insulate the entire heap to keep it hot.
11. Turn the heap, sides to middle, when it starts to cool (usually after a week), so that all parts get 'peak heated'.

Peak heated compost

These graphs illustrate the effect of nitrogen activators, particle size, volume, and turning, on the heating of compost.

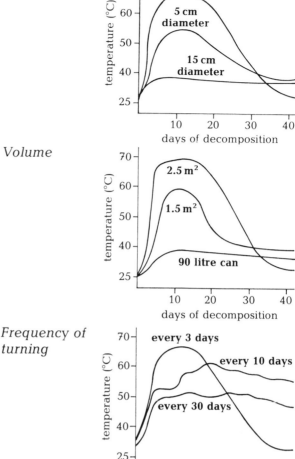

Particle size

Volume

Frequency of turning

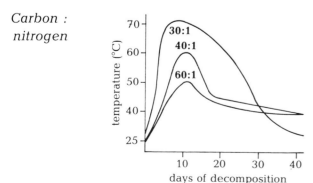

Carbon : nitrogen

The fire-lighters

Compounds that are rich in nitrogen are known as activators, and these lower the carbon-nitrogen ratio in a heap, making it heat up more quickly. A high proportion of carbon to nitrogen is still required (about 20 or 30:1) otherwise the heap will get very slimy, and can even catch fire. The carbon gives 'substance' to the finished compost.

The pernicious weeds

Tenacious perennials with tough underground parts have a tendency to regrow if put on the compost. Dock roots actually contain chemical inhibitors to prevent soil bacteria and fungi breaking them down. However, these roots are far too good to waste. Rhizomes of couch can be baked and then added. Otherwise, try making your own 'silage' with weed roots in black plastic bags, and add this to the compost after a year.

Presowing cultivations

Many weeds can be controlled by cultivating the ground correctly before you plant it up or lay a lawn. There are many methods from which to choose, depending on the weeds present and the type of planting that you may wish to carry out. A few ideas are outlined here.

The stale seedbed technique

This is a good way of tricking the annual weeds. In the spring make a seedbed in the normal way, only do it a couple of weeks earlier than usual.

● Fork the ground over.

● Rake to remove stones, lumps and create a fine tilth. Then, instead of putting your seeds in, leave it. If the weather is cold, then cover the bed with a clear material, such as glass, plastic or polypropylene fleece. Many annual weeds, stimulated by the light and warmth, will start to grow.

● After two weeks, hoe them off and put in your seeds. They will germinate quickly, benefiting from the warmth and lack of competition. This method is sometimes referred to as a weed strike.

Rotovating

This method can be used to clear a plot that contains many perennial weeds, but it will take a few months so be patient.

Rotovating a plot once will cause perennial weeds to spread and regenerate, increasing the weed problem. However, if several passes are made over a period of time, repeatedly destroying the foliage that the fragments send up, then the perennials will eventually become exhausted and die.

The best time to do this is between April and June when, hopefully, the soil is moist or fairly dry.

● Rotovate to 2 cm depth.
● After two weeks, rotovate to 4 cm depth.
● After two weeks, rotovate to 6 cm depth.
● After two weeks, rotovate to 8 cm depth.

If the rotovator has different speeds, then use the highest speed for the rotor blades to chop and tear the weeds. After six weeks the weed roots will be very weak, and will start to give in.

Rotovating soil is very bad for the structure, destroying surface tilth and causing compaction below the depth of the blades. To remedy this, sow a deep-rooting, fast-growing green manure, such as winter grazing rye, after rotovating for the last time. The roots will relieve compaction, help to build up the soil structure and suppress any fragments of weak weed growth still trying to get through.

Although this method puts the garden out of action over the summer, it is well worth it. I have cleared an allotment plot of creeping thistle and docks in this way and have had little trouble with them since.

Digging in the dark!

Scientists in Europe have shown that annual weed problems are greatly reduced if cultivations are done in the dark! Many weed seeds are 'photo-induced' and germinate after they receive a flash of light. This is why the stale seedbed technique works. Trials on farms have shown that the numbers of cleavers, chickweed and fat hen plants are dramatically reduced when cultivations are carried out at night, and the emergence of wild chamomile and small toadflax are stopped completely.

If you try this and get caught out by a neighbour, then tell them to come and see the results a few months later! A farmer in Germany has been using this method for years and has very few weeds in his crops.

Altering the soil conditions

Many weeds grow best in certain types of soils, e.g. coltsfoot thrives in badly drained soils. So, to get rid of coltsfoot, one method is to improve the drainage. Another example is spurrey, which grows on lime-deficient ground. To eradicate this one, you've guessed it, add lime to neutralise the soil.

Stripping off the top

Stripping off the top few centimetres gives quick results when clearing an infected plot but is not a method to be recommended. Deep-rooting weeds will soon appear from fragmented pieces of root and a lot of fertile topsoil will have been wasted. If this method is used, then replace the soil removed with organic matter and stack the weedy soil for two years to give loam for potting composts.

Double digging

In double digging, the soil is turned over and weeds buried upside-down. It is a very satisfying method and can transform a weedy patch. Details on double digging are given in my companion book in this series, *Soil Care and Management*.

Words of warning:

● Do not mix the topsoil with the subsoil.

● Weeds may decompose, anaerobically producing toxins, so do not plant deep-rooting crops immediately.

● Ensure perennial weeds are buried to a depth of at least 15 cm or they will soon emerge.

Alternatively, especially if you have a bed of couch, you can fork the patch over and remove roots and rhizomes by hand. A 'twitch rake' can be used to remove couch. This can be made easily by drilling holes in a rake and welding in 15 cm nails; a formidable weapon against weeds!

Planting effectively

Modules

Garden plants can compete far more effectively against weed seedlings if they are given a head start. It is relatively simple to raise plants in modules instead of sowing seeds directly in the ground.

Polystyrene or plastic modules come in a variety of sizes and are available from most garden centres. If you do not like the idea of using plastic, then you can make your own modules:

● By wrapping newspaper around a cylinder and twisting at the end to make a biodegradable pot.

● By using the cardboard tubes from inside toilet rolls.

● By dispensing with containers altogether and using a special blocking tool to compress 'blocking' compost into cubes. This is well worth the initial expense.

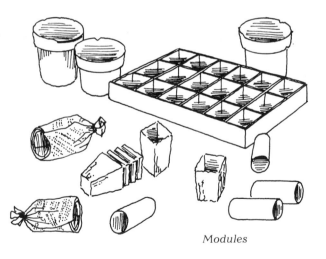

Modules

Use a proprietary organic seed compost or make your own, e.g. 3 buckets cocopeat, 1 bucket coarse sand, ½ bucket compost or worm-casts, 80 g calcified seaweed (dolomite lime). The better the compost the healthier the plant, and stronger growing plants can grow away from the weeds.

Spacing

Close planting of vegetables and annuals can keep light from the soil and suppress many weeds, particularly annuals. The type of light that filters through leaves can actually promote dormancy of some weed seeds.

Vegetable plants can be set out in blocks rather than rows. As well as suppressing weeds, this type of planting makes the fullest use of the land and reduces the competition between plants.

Periwinkle

The spacing given below will provide maximum crop yields under ideal conditions.

Plants	Cm between plants (average figure)
Beetroot (multi-sown)	20
Broad beans	22.5
Brussels sprouts	50–90
Summer cabbages	35
Winter cabbages	45
Calabrese	25
Carrots	10
Cauliflowers – summer	52.5
autumn	67.5
winter	75
French beans	25
Potatoes	55

The closer the planting, the smaller the individual plants. Crops such as onions have little or no weed-suppressing effect. Vegetables which require a large spacing, such as winter cauliflowers and Brussels sprouts, can be intercropped with a quick-maturing crop. Hearting lettuce is a suitable catch crop, and can be planted in April and cleared in mid-June. This will maximise the use of space as well as creating ground cover to control weed growth. Remember to choose a catch crop that is fast growing, as, if it starts to compete with the main crop, then it becomes a weed in its own right.

Ground cover

In the ornamental garden, vigorous-growing ground-cover plants help to suppress weeds. There are many low-growing plants available and several different species can be planted together to give a mosaic of colours and leaf textures.

Suitable ground-cover plants include:

Alchemilla mollis: sun or shade.

Anthemis nobilis: dry, sandy conditions. Evergreen.

Arctostaphylos uva-ursi: acid soil, sun or light shade. Evergreen.

Asarum europaeum: cool, moist shade. Evergreen.

Ballota pseudodictamnus: full sun, well-drained site. Evergreen.

Bergenia spp.: sun or shade. Evergreen.

Brunnera macrophylla: cool, moist shade.

Campanula portenschlagiana: rich soil, sunny site.

Ceanothus thyrsiflorus repens: sunny bank. Evergreen.

Cerastium tomentosum: sunny, dry site. Evergreen.

Convallaria majalis: moist shade.

Cotoneaster 'Gnome': sun or shade. Evergreen.

Duchesnea indica: well-drained soil.

Euonymus fortunei var. radicans: well-drained site. Evergreen.

Galeobdolon argentatum: cool, moist soil. Evergreen and invasive.

Gaultheria procumbens: cool, moist shade, acid soil. Evergreen.

Hedera canariensis, Hedera helix, Hedera colchica: sun or shade. Evergreen and invasive.

Hosta sieboldiana: moist shade.

Hypericum calycinum: sandy soil. Evergreen and invasive.

Lamium maculatum: shade.

Nepeta × *fassenii*: sun, well-drained soil.

Pachysandra terminalis: dry shade. Evergreen.

Phlox spp.: sun, well-drained soil.

Pulmonaria angustifolia: shade.

Stachys byzantina: full sun, well-drained soil. Evergreen.

Vancouveria hexandra: humus-rich soil, shady site.

Vinca major, Vinca minor: sun or shade. Evergreen and invasive.

Waldsteinia ternata: any soil, sun or shade. Evergreen and invasive.

One of the most effective ground-cover plants is grass. This can be used effectively under fruit and specimen trees to control weeds (when mown regularly). An area of approximately 1 m^2 around each plant should be mulched to prevent competition, see below.

Whatever you plant, it is important to:

● Prepare the site well beforehand, removing any weeds.

● Plant vigorous, healthy plants at the right time so that they can compete effectively with the weeds.

Mulches

Mulching means covering the ground. Plants need light to grow and if this is excluded with a mulch, then they will gradually die. Mulches can be used in a variety of ways:

● To clear a plot, if you have time to wait but not time for the hard labour!

● To control weeds in one part of the garden while you are concentrating on another.

● To place around established plants, such as shrubs, to prevent competition from weeds.

● To plant through, for weed-free growth.

● To cover paths and other areas to be kept weed-free.

As well as controlling weeds, mulches have several other beneficial effects, such as:

● Retaining moisture.

● Altering the temperature of the soil and the air just above it.

● Helping the soil structure.

● Adding nutrients to the soil (if a biodegradable mulch is used).

● Helping to keep the crops clean and free of disease.

How to apply

Always apply a mulch to warm, moist soil to keep it that way. If the soil is dry, then water it before applying the mulch.

If the mulch used is 'bitty' and not sappy,

such as wood chips, straw and leaf mould, then the thicker the layer the better. These mulches work better on annual than on perennial weeds, as plants such as dandelion can easily force their way through. Take care when mulching trees and shrubs. Many of these plants are grafted and if the mulch is piled above the graft union, then the top part (or 'scion') may root, which may alter the characteristics of the plant. Even if there is no graft, mulching around a stem may encourage pests and rotting.

When using thick sheet mulches, such as carpet, anchor them down with wire pegs. These can be made easily from pieces of coat hanger. Thin sheet mulches may rip if pegged in, so these are better weighted with stones or dug into the soil at the edges. If the mulch is not permeable, then bank up the soil slightly underneath it so that any water runs to the edges. You can 'kill two birds with one stone' in this way, by laying a black plastic mulch over a slight mound of soil between rows of runner beans. The weeds will be controlled and run off water will water these moisture-loving plants. Mulch mats can be made from squares of black plastic, 1.2 m^2. Cut a slit in the plastic, place it around the (watered) tree and dig it in or weight it at the edges. Vegetable crops and 'whips' used for making a hedge can be planted through slits in sheet mulches, even before the ground beneath is totally weed-free.

Mulches used for ground clearance are best used when the weeds are trying to grow. If laid in the spring, then most annuals and shallow-rooting perennials will be dead by late autumn. It may take longer than a year to clear deep-rooting weeds, such as bindweed, dock and dandelion, and those with corms (bulbous buttercup) or bulbils (oxalis) can be very persistent.

Caring for mulched plants

Watering and feeding mulched plants need not be a problem. Water well and apply a slow-release fertiliser, such as compost, under a mulch. Any subsequent watering and liquid feeding can be done through the slits. It is possible to lay dribble lines or 'leaky' pipes under mulches to liquid feed and water permanently mulched plants.

Mulches

Black plastic

Dense woven plastic

Carpet

Cardboard

Newspaper

Compost

Well-rotted manure

Hay

Mulch	Use
Black plastic Available in several thicknesses. 150 gauge (38 mm) – thin, like a dustbin bag, will only last one season, 300 gauge or thicker – will last longer. Non-biodegradable.	● Good for land clearance and eradicating perennials. ● Most plants, from vegetable seedlings to trees, can be planted through it. ● As a mulch mat around trees and shrubs.
Black woven plastic Dense enough to keep down weeds but porous to air and water. Non-biodegradable. Can fray and release 'plastic strings' which can get tangled around plants and wildlife.	● Excellent for permanent plantings, as plants can be fed and watered. ● Use to stand pots of plants on outside. ● Do not use for permanent planting where couch is a problem, as rhizomes can pierce it and mat into it.
Non-woven fleece A thin, non-biodegradable material.	● Use in conjunction with mulches such as wood bark, to prevent the latter becoming incorporated into the soil.
Carpet Only use heavier wool and hessian-backed carpets. They will suppress weeds for at least a season and then rot down slowly.	● Good for land clearance. ● Can be used on paths and covered with wood chips or bark for aesthetic reasons.
Cardboard Use flattened cardboard boxes and overlap the edges. Biodegradable.	● Good for land clearance. ● Use as mulch mats around woody perennials.
Compressed peat paper Usually available on a roll, like a stiff brown paper. Made of compressed peat and cellulose (from recycled cardboard boxes). Rots quickly. Can bleach and, therefore, prevent warming of soil. Shrinks when wetted. Tends to rip and blow away.	● Use on vegetable beds and transplant plants through it. ● Keeps weeds down for two to three months. ● Apply water, and allow to dry before planting to prevent decapitation of transplants. ● Can be used under another mulch, such as straw, to prolong life and reduce the amount of straw required.
Newspaper Only use black and white newspaper, as colour supplements contain some heavy metals. Several thicknesses are required. Biodegradable, but fairly long lasting as the paper hardens if exposed to the elements.	● Use on paths. ● Use around perennial plants. ● Use in conjunction with other biodegradable mulches to make them go further.
Compost Provides nutrients. Usually too valuable to use as a thick layer.	● Use on vegetable crops with a long growing period.
Well-rotted manure As above. Lasts longer and provides more organic matter if composted. Less danger of 'burning' plants and leaching of nutrients if composted.	● On heavy feeders, such as blackcurrants. ● Reduces blackspot on roses as it prevents splashback of spores onto underside of leaves.
Hay Provides nutrients. Biodegradable. Insulates soil. Can introduce weed seeds.	● Use around fruit trees and bushes. ● Can be used on beds if planted with transplants after hay has rotted down.

Straw

Leaf mould

Lawn mowings

Forest bark

Sawdust

Shredded prunings/wood chips

Mushroom compost

Gravel

Mulch	Use
Straw Longer lasting than hay. Can cause nitrogen robbery if incorporated. May contain herbicide residues. Partially rotted straw is preferable as it does not blow away! Can add potassium to the soil. Biodegradable.	• Use around perennials. • Use under plants such as strawberries and courgettes to keep the fruit clean. • Use on potatoes instead of earthing up. • Can place comfrey or nettle leaves beneath it to prevent nitrogen robbery. • Can use on paths between beds, but attracts slugs and may cause nitrogen robbery from the edge of beds.
Leaf mould Free! Slowly provides humus and nutrients. Stack leaves in bins to rot. Allow rainwater to wash airborne lead from those gathered in urban areas.	• An attractive mulch to use around perennials and annuals. • Can be a bit slippery for use on paths (also a waste of valuable organic matter).
Peat A non-renewable resource and environmentally unacceptable.	• Do not use.
Lawn mowings A nutrient-rich mulch. Does not cause nitrogen robbery. Can introduce weed seeds. Biodegradable.	• Spread thinly and top up, or it may heat up excessively. • Use around annuals and perennials. • Very useful around onions to control weeds and feed the crop.
Forest bark Attractive, biodegradable. Long lasting! Usually bought composted to remove pathogens and resins. Check source to ensure no herbicides or weedkillers have been used. Phenols and tannins may help control weeds, pests and diseases.	• Use on established plants only. • Apply over another mulch to prevent incorporation and nitrogen robbery. • Attractive around ornamentals.
Sawdust Can cause nitrogen robbery. Can 'cake' and repel water. Check source to ensure pesticides are not found on wood.	• Use on paths so that there is no danger of nitrogen robbery.
Shredded prunings/wood chips Free (if you have access to a shredder).	• Use around trees and shrubs. • Do not apply shredded prunings around the parent plant or there may be a risk of spreading disease.
Mushroom compost Use organic mushroom compost only. Other mushroom composts contain pesticide residues. *Not acidic*, contains large amounts of chalk.	• Use around annuals and perennials. • Do not use on acid-loving plants, such as rhododendrons and azaleas.
Slates, gravel Non-biodegradable, but not harmful to the environment.	• Attractive mulch on paths, alpine and 'scree' gardens. • Can be used on herb beds.

Green manures

A green manure is a plant that is grown for the purpose of incorporating into the soil. The cultivation of green manures is dealt with in the companion volume in this series, *How to make your Garden Fertile* by Pauline Pears. Many green manures can be used as a living mulch, helping to suppress weeds:

● Grazing rye (*Secale cereale*) is a good weed suppressant, survives on moist soil types and can be used in conjunction with cultivation to clear a plot of persistent perennial weeds, see page 46.

● Leguminous green manures, such as trefoil (*Medicago lupulina*) or clover (*Trifolium pratense*), can be used as a ground cover under tall, widely spaced crops, such as sweet corn and Brussels sprouts, to suppress weeds.

● Phacelia (*Phacelia tanactifolia*) can be grown as a ground cover between well-established shrubs if it is cut regularly to prevent competition.

Grazing rye

Trefoil

Clover

Phacelia

Crop rotation

Crop rotation can help to control weeds as well as pests and diseases. Weed-susceptible crops can be alternated with weed-suppressing crops. A possible four year rotation is outlined below and another possible rotation, for a small garden, is shown in the photograph below.

In the four year rotation, the potatoes and green manures act as weed-suppressing crops. The miscellaneous vegetables, such as courgettes, squashes and pumpkins, could be fitted in to give a five year rotation and would also act as a good ground-cover crop.

Crop rotation helps to control weeds most effectively if used in conjunction with close planting, mulching and the deep bed system.

Year	Crop	Additions to the soil	Other information
1	Potatoes/tomatoes, possibly followed by a green manure, e.g. rye.	Manure/compost.	Covers soil, protecting structure and suppressing weeds.
2	Peas/beans, possibly followed by a green manure.	None (as these crops fix their own nitrogen).	Peas and beans are susceptible to weed competition. The green manure covers the soil over winter and suppresses weeds.
3	Brassicas.	Lime, e.g. ground dolomitic limestone or calcified seaweed.	Can be undersown with a leguminous green manure to protect soil and suppress weeds.
4	Roots/onions, followed by a quick-growing green manure, such as mustard, before returning to potatoes.		Deep rooting. Susceptible to competition from weeds. Carrots are less susceptible if close planted on a bed system.

Four newly constructed raised beds ready for planting in a rotation

Raised beds

Raised beds help to control weeds in a number of ways:

● They are not cultivated so dormant weed seeds are not exposed to light and stimulated to germinate.

● Perennial weeds can be pulled out of the well-structured soil easily by hand, without damaging adjoining plants.

● Beds can be completely mulched and planted up with modules, suppressing any annual weed growth.

● No rows are required as beds are not walked on, and plants can be positioned to smother out weeds and maximise use of space, see page 48.

● Beds are 'discreet' units and can be worked on and weeded one at a time; far more satisfying than a seemingly endless garden.

The construction of deep beds involves digging over the entire plot, then marking out beds approximately 120 cm wide with paths 45 cm wide. The soil from the paths is then placed onto the beds. The beds should run from north to south to receive maximum daylight. Paths can be kept weed-free by mulching with carpets or straw. Personally, I find that this attracts slugs, so I usually hoe the compacted paths every few weeks. This is more useful than digging out any perennials in the paths as the tops of the weeds regenerate and can be composted, thus making use of the nutrients in the path soil.

Hygiene

Once you have got rid of your own weeds, you need to keep your garden free from unwelcome visitors. New weeds will be most eager to move in as seed or creeping vegetative roots, rhizomes and runners.

Seeds
Many airborne seeds can be kept out by fences and hedges around your garden or allotment. A little tact also helps. I once collected all my neighbour's coltsfoot flowers before they set seed, by making the excuse

that I wanted to make some wine. The wine was very nice and I had far fewer coltsfoot seedlings in the garden the following year.

Some seeds stick to clothing and fur, and can get into the garden on people and animals. I do not suggest making the garden a no-go area! However, it can be fun seeing what seeds come in in this way. The weed population in my garden changes according to the other gardens in which I work. After working in an old walled garden, mullien, alkanet and poppies began to spring up on my own site. This was quite a welcome change from the coltsfoot and couch which had been eradicated the year before. A weed expert and enthusiast, Sir Edward Salisbury, once grew over 300 weeds, representing 20 different species, from debris removed from his trouser turn-ups. Another 'weed' researcher, H.T. Clifford, grew 43 species of weed, one quarter of which were grasses, on mud scraped from his shoes!

Weed seeds can also get into the garden in manures, having survived passing through an animal's gut. Heating the manure by composting can destroy many weed seeds. However, some seed types can survive the heat treatment, and blackberry pips can even germinate from the boiled pulp left over from jelly making.

The creeping weeds

Creeping roots, rhizomes and runners can be kept at bay with a barrier. If your garden is surrounded by a fence, then dig a trench beneath it removing up to 15 cm of the subsoil, and attach heavy gauge polythene to

Attaching polythene to fence

the bottom of the fence reaching down into the trench. Personally, I am not keen on plastic in the garden and have used breeze blocks and slates under the fence. It really keeps the ground elder and ivy at bay. By keeping perennials away from the boundaries the slug and snail problem is also greatly reduced, as these pests tend to hide in the perennial weeds and venture out to eat your plants at night. Many allotments are not allowed fences. In this case, simply dig a trench around the edge, but be sure to put up signs or cover the trench with planks as you want to keep the weeds out and not injure your fellow gardeners!

Finally, when you bring in new perennial plants, always check the roots for pieces of weed root or stem, such as field bindweed or ground elder. A little vigilance at this stage may save you a lifetime's weeding.

Removing weeds

Despite all efforts to keep your plot weed-free, seedlings and perennials will inevitably appear. It is important to get the tenacious ones as early as you can before they grow and spread. There are several methods that you can use.

Hoeing

This is the quickest way of getting rid of annual seedlings as the roots do not regenerate. Hoeing will only kill persistent perennial weeds if you prevent them from getting above the soil surface. In hoeing, the blade is moved back and forth parallel to the soil surface but just beneath it, to cut off seedlings at ground level.

Points to remember:

● Keep the blade sharp, so that it cuts cleanly and works at a shallow depth.

● Ideally, hoe when it is dry and sunny but while there is still moisture just below the surface. If the hoe is used on wet soil, then the weeds can just reroot again.

● A hoe can be used between plants or rows of plants, to clear an area before planting or even on gravel paths and driveways.

● Hoe regularly when weeds are small.

● Do not hoe oxalis, it only encourages it!

● Take care to avoid root damage when hoeing near shallow-rooted crops.

● Timing is important when hoeing perennials, e.g. if creeping thistle is hoed off in spring, then it will only cause the plant to regenerate. It is best to follow the old rhyme:

> 'Stub a thistle in May, it will be back
>   the next day,
> Stub a thistle in June, it will be back soon,
> Stub a thistle in July, it will surely die.'

This is because the food reserves in the roots are depleted during the season in order to feed the flower stem.

● Excessive hoeing can be harmful, drying out moist soils and damaging structure, so do not be over-vigilant.

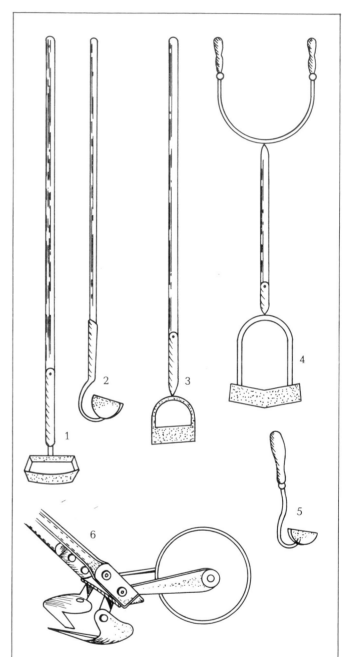

1. *Reciprocating hoe*: use with push/pull action as blade is pivoted.
2. *Draw hoe*: pull hoe.
3. *Dutch hoe*: push action.
4. *Lincolnshire longhorn*: good for clearing land.
5. *Onion hoe*: useful on beds for hoeing around closely spaced plants.
6. *Wheel hoe*: much quicker and easier than the Dutch hoe, especially in long lines of row crops. Blades can be adjusted to the width between rows of plants.

Hand weeding

Many weeds can be removed by hand, which can be relaxing and therapeutic or back-breaking! Deep beds and light soils are easier to weed in this way. Many annuals, such as bittercress, shepherd's purse, groundsel and fat hen, are worth hand pulling (before they set seed). In friable, deep soils even some perennials can be pulled out. Docks do not regenerate readily if the top 15 cm of the root is removed. Hand weeding should not be underrated as it is thorough, precise and less damaging to neighbouring plants than many other methods.

Flame weeding

Flame weeding is a more gentle method of weed control than it sounds. The weeds do not need to be totally incinerated. The idea is to pass the flame over them until they turn darker or brighter green. This bursts the plants' cell walls and they will then die. Small seedlings will die very quickly but perennials may need several 'blasts' once a week until the roots are exhausted.

Where to use your flame weeder:

- On paths and driveways.
- On walls and round the edges of the house.
- To weed the seedbed before seedlings emerge.
- Between rows of vegetables.

A tip for your seedbed. Place a piece of glass over one part of the row. When your seedlings emerge under the glass (two to three days ahead of the rest), pass the flame weeder over the soil to kill off the weeds, before the majority of your seedlings come up. Crops such as onions and sweet corn can be flame weeded quickly when they are growing without damage. Research has also shown that flame weeding strawberries before the buds have formed reduces the risk of botrytis and increases the sugar content of the crop. Do not make your own flame weeder. It is safer to purchase one from a reputable garden centre, either fuelled by paraffin or propane gas.

Novel ideas

One day, amateur gardeners may be able to use biological weed controls.

- At present, the biological control of weeds by parasites and disease pathogens is being actively explored by scientists. For example, there is a possibility of using the larvae of a South African moth to control the tenacious weed, bracken. These methods must be approached with extreme caution, however, as there may be a danger of upsetting the ecological balance if a foreign species is introduced.
- Domestic animals, such as geese, ducks and chickens, have been used in woody perennial beds to control weeds, but there is a danger of soil compaction.
- Some plants have also been tried as weed-deterrent species. *Tagetes minuta* is a tall, half-hardy plant that is suggested as a control for couch and ground elder. Tomato plants and wormwood are also reputed to slow down the growth of neighbouring plants, including the weeds. This is called 'allelopathy'. These methods have not been proven, but are well worth a try in the garden if all else fails.

Weed control on the lawn

A weedy lawn

If you look closely at the lawn, then you will find that in most cases the sward consists of a whole range of plants, both grasses and broad-leaved species. This is usually acceptable to the organic gardener as it will support a great variety of wildlife. A mixture of species will also keep the lawn looking healthier and ensure a green covering in different situations. For example:

● Meadow grasses grow in the shade.
● Clover will grow in soils poor in nitrogen.
● Yarrow will survive in dry conditions.

You may even like to create a meadow in part of the lawned area.

● For flowers to compete with grasses in a meadow an infertile soil is required, so remove grass mowings for a year or remove a little of the topsoil and use elsewhere in the garden.

● Raise flowers in pots, choosing meadow species that are suitable for your soil type.

● Sow the site with a mixture of fine grass species suitable for your soil (after preparing a seedbed).

● Plant out the flowers in clumps amongst the grasses to give them a head start.

● For a spring meadow, mow from July onwards. Suitable species include: lady's smock, cowslip, lesser stitchwort, self-heal, bugle, daisy, cat's-ear, rough hawkbit, dandelion, yellow rattle, salad burnet.

● For a summer meadow, mow until June and again in late September. Suitable species include: knapweed, lady's bedstraw, sheep's sorrel, field scabious, ox-eye daisy, meadow buttercup, yarrow, devil's bit scabious, perforated St John's wort, goatsbeard.

● Mow paths amidst the meadow to make it accessible and attractive.

So, the main advice for weeding a lawn is do not. If you do want a pure grass lawn, then the table outlines the control of the more tenacious weeds. Do not use weedkillers on the lawn. It is a place of recreation and pleasure not poisons.

Moss taking over a lawn

Weed	Control	Weed	Control
Clover, medick, trefoil	Feed with a nitrogen-rich fertiliser in the spring, and top-dress in the autumn (2:4:1 – sand, loam, leaf mould) to improve the soil. Mow with the grass-box on the mower to remove seeds. Rake the turf and lift stems before mowing.	**Broad-leaved perennial grasses, e.g. Yorkshire fog**	Survive regular mowing. Dig up small patches by hand and reseed or turf. In large areas, cut the clumps with a knife or edging tool before mowing to reduce the strength.
Daisy	A common weed where soil is compacted, the pH is high and the lawn has been mown too short. Therefore, eliminate the causes.	**Woodrush, sheep's sorrel**	Appearance of these weeds, together with sparse grass, indicates high acidity. Apply ground limestone in the autumn or winter at a rate of 70 g/sq m.
Thistle, plantain, dandelion, self-heal	Hand weed or cut below the surface with an old kitchen knife. Spot treatment with salt is effective in some cases but treated areas will need resowing after the salt has been leached out.	**Mind your own business** (*Soleirolia soleirolii*)	Hoe if dry. Hand weed if wet. Flame weed patches and reseed.
Yarrow	Improve general lawn care.	**Parsley piert, pearlwort**	Control by encouraging vigour in the turf, by feeding and top-dressing. Also, irrigate in dry periods. Do not mow the grass too short as this encourages these weeds.
Moss	Found on waterlogged sites. Also a problem on fertile sandy soils, acid soils, in shade when grass is mown too short and as a result of periods of summer drought. Therefore, eliminate the appropriate problem. Remove patches of dead moss by raking and resow immediately with grass seed to prevent weeds getting in.	**Mouse-ear hawkweed, creeping buttercup, common mouse-ear chickweed**	In spring, lift stolons with a wire-toothed rake, then cut with a mower.
Annual meadow-grass	Large patches of this weed are a nuisance as they are susceptible to disease and drought. To remove, deal with compaction problems, reduce shade and keep the grass-box on the mower to remove seed-heads when mowing.	**Slender speedwell**	Rake before mowing. Compost mowings, as speedwell can regenerate from stem sections scattered by the mower.

Woody weeds

Trees and other woody perennials are a real asset in the garden but sometimes need to be kept under control.

Tree seedlings

Tree seeds come into the garden on the wind or are carried in by animals. Seedlings from wind-carried seeds, such as sycamore and ash, usually cause the most problem.

● Dig up as soon as possible, as the seedlings develop strong taproots when they are no more than a few centimetres high. Replant in a suitable site.

Tree seedlings taking over

Tree suckers

Many garden trees and shrubs produce suckers, e.g. poplar, lilac, sumach, dogwood and myrobalan (a rootstock commonly used for flowering cherries, plums and almonds).

● Remove suckers with a sharp knife, secateurs or small saw. Cut as close to the point of origin as you can, if possible severing the shoot flush with the root from which it has grown.

Brambles

● Grub out shoot tips that have rooted where they touch the ground.

● Cut back top growth before attempting to get out the roots.

Goats really do eat brambles!

● Employ a goat (I inherited a garden of brambles and a goat did all the hard work for me in six months).

Bamboo

● Cut back invasive clumps to ground level in April. Use canes elsewhere in the garden!

Ivy

Ivy does not harm walls if the brickwork is sound, but if not kept in check, then it can damage guttering and enhance the 'crumbling' of crumbly walls. Ivy does not kill healthy trees but it can hide damage on trees and may catch the wind in a storm, enhancing storm damage.

● If ivy is causing a problem, then sever at ground level. Do not remove it if it is doing no harm as it is a haven for wildlife, providing food and shelter.

When you have read this book, hopefully you will not regard so many of the plants in the garden as weeds. If you come to understand your weeds, then you can control them more easily, but please leave a few for the wildlife. Weeds are incredibly successful plants and, in their place, deserve to be treated with respect.

Trouble shooting

This table summarises the methods of weed control
that can be applied in different situations.

Situation	Weed control	Page
The neglected patch	● Mulch.	49–51
	● Rotovate successively, and follow with a green manure.	46, 52
	● Alter soil conditions.	47
	● Dig and remove weeds by hand.	57
	Then:	
	● Use well-composted organic matter.	44–45
	● Maintain crop cover.	48–49
	● Initially, plant through mulches.	49–51
	● Plant a clearing crop, such as potatoes. Potatoes will not clear couch.	53
Seedbeds	● Use a stale seedbed technique.	46
	● Hoe.	56
	● Flame weed.	57
	● Maintain cover with mulches or green manures when not in use.	49–52
	● Hygiene.	54–55
Annual beds	● Prepare site well before planting.	46–47
	● Use a stale seedbed technique.	46
	● Hoe.	56
	● Flame weed.	57
	● Plant through mulches.	49–51
	● Maintain ground cover by closely spacing plants and using green manures.	48–49, 52
	● Adopt a suitable rotation.	53
	● Hand weed.	57
	● Use well-composted organic matter.	44–45
	● Prevent weeds coming in from outside.	54–55
	● Disturb soil as little as possible when planting annuals.	47
	● Plant annuals at the correct time.	47
	● Use healthy plants.	47, 55
Perennial beds	● Prepare the plot and remove weeds before planting.	46–47
	● Plant through a mulch.	49–51
	● Use ground cover beneath plants.	48–49
	● Ensure that plants do not have weed roots with them when planting.	55
	● Use healthy stock.	47, 55
	● Keep on top of weeds when they appear by hoeing and/or hand weeding (avoid hoeing around surface-rooting perennial plants).	56–57
Lawns	● Follow a programme of good lawn maintenance.	58–59
	● Hand weed.	57
Paths	● Remove all weeds before laying a path.	46–47, 56–57
	● Place a mulch, such as woven black plastic, beneath wood chip and gravel paths.	49–51, 54
	● Good path construction.	49
	● Hoe.	56
	● Hand weed.	57
	● Flame weed.	57
Woody weeds	● Cut back if they are causing a problem.	60

Glossary

Alkaloid: a class of plant products that are usually poisonous.

Allelopathy: the release of a chemical by a plant that inhibits the growth of nearby plants.

Awn: a stiff bristle-like projection, usually at the tip of an organ.

Bulbil: a small bulb that develops from an aerial bud.

Catch crop: a fast-growing crop used to fill in temporary gaps.

Clearing crop: a crop that cleans the land of weeds.

Compaction: where soil is packed down due to weight from above.

Compost activator: a substance containing nitrogen, bacteria or herbs that speeds up the composting process.

Corm: a type of underground swollen stem.

Double digging: cultivating the soil to a depth of two spits (a spit is the depth of a spade).

Dribble line: a type of plant irrigation where water drips out of holes along a pipe.

Earthing up: heaping earth up around the base of a plant.

Fruiting bodies: a part of the plant which produces fruit.

Garden escape: a plant originally introduced into gardens.

Green manure: a crop that is grown to incorporate into the soil.

Grub out: dig up and remove roots and stumps.

Herbicide: a chemical weedkiller.

Humus: a formless, black, jelly-like substance containing a wide range of complex life chemicals. The main breakdown product of organic matter.

Hybridize: to produce an individual plant from genetically different parents.

Midrib: the central vein in a leaf.

Nitrogen robbery: removal of nitrogen from the soil by soil life.

Node: a point on the plant stem from which one or more leaves arise.

Ochrea: a tube around the stem at the leaf base.

Organic: a method of growing plants which avoids the use of chemical pesticides and artificial fertilisers.

Organic matter: composed of the remains of dead plants and animals.

pH: a measure of the acidity of the soil. A pH of 7 is taken to be neutral; a soil with a pH of less than 7 is said to be acid, while a pH figure of more than 7 is said to be alkaline.

Plant nutrient: any of the mineral substances that are absorbed by the roots of plants for nourishment.

Rhizome: an underground horizontal stem.

Rootstock: a plant which provides the roots for another variety of the same plant, which is grafted on to it.

Rosette: a plant with leaves that radiate out from a short stem at soil level.

Runner: a creeping stem that arises from a bud and runs along the ground.

Scion: a shoot or bud from one plant grafted to another.

Scree garden: a garden based on rock.

Stale seedbed technique: cultivating the seedbed to stimulate weed growth, which can then be hoed off before planting seeds.

Stolon: a branch that bends to the ground and consequently roots.

Sward: a mixture of grasses.

Taproot: a persistent, robust primary root.

Tilth: a fine, crumbly surface layer of soil.

Twitch rake: a rake with long teeth.

Umbellifer: a family of plants that includes cow parsley, carrot and hemlock.

Whip: young tree.

Index